THE SECRETS OF META COSMIC PROJECTION

PARKER
PUBLISHING COMPANY

All rights reserved. No part of this publication may be reproduced without the prior permission of the copyright owner.

The views and ideas expressed in this book are the personal opinions of the author, and do not necessarily represent the views of the Publisher.

Library of Congress Catalogin in Publication Data

Secrets of meta-cosmic projection.

1.success. 2. Psychical research.

© Copyright 1977 by PARKER PUBLISHING COMPANY

Contact us: info@parkerpub.co

www.parkerpub.co

THE SECRETS OF META COSMIC PROJECTION

What This Book Can Do For You

Would you like to know the secrets that can bring into your life all you need and want? Would you like to have the money to pay off bills, buy a house, purchase a car, travel, and still have a healthy bank account? Do you or a loved one have a health problem you want cured? Is depression or emotional stress a problem in your life? The secrets of Meta-Cosmic Projection can banish these problems and more for you — not in years or months but *now!*

Have you had a problem finding a job? Do you want a promotion at work? Would you like to have better working conditions? The secrets of Meta-Cosmic Projection can bring you the future you want by solving your problems today. Countless numbers of people have already discovered the unlimited power these secrets place in their life and you owe it to yourself to discover those secrets too. The invincible force of Meta-Cosmic Projection has worked miracles in the lives of thousands, and it can work miracles in your life today.

Forty-five Ways This Book Can Help You

Here is a partial list of the case histories that you will read about in the following chapters. All of these people have used the secrets of Meta-Cosmic Projection to bring into their life the things and goals they wanted and needed. The miraculous techniques that allowed them to do this are available to you in the pages of this book. You can use the irresistible power of the Psychic Binocular technique; the impenetrable force of the Meta-Psychic Shield technique; the miraculous power of the Psychic Organizer technique; the unlimited power of many

Meta-Cosmic Projection techniques; the limitless power of the Meta-Cosmic Microphone technique and the supreme force of the Meta-Cosmic Projection Telephone technique today and have everything you want and need.

They Did It and So Can You!

1. Calvin and Doris G. needed $10,000 — they received much more. *(Chapter 14)*
2. Mike N. got the money he needed to pay his bills and make a down payment on a new house. *(Chapter 14)*
3. Emily V. banished asthma attacks. *(Chapter 7)*
4. John B. cured his wife's stomach ulcers. *(Chapter 7)*
5. Phyllis H. overcame arthritis. *(Chapter 7)*
6. Tom K. won a color T.V. *(Chapter 5)*
7. Ron O. got the new car he wanted. *(Chapter 5)*
8. Dan and Iris B. built their dream house. *(Chapter 5)*
9. Cecil G. saved his son's life and helped put two dope pushers in jail. *(Chapter 8)*
10. Sharon A. stopped a burglar and kept her family and home safe. *(Chapter 8)*
11. Victor M. regained the use of his right arm. *(Chapter 7)*
12. Donald W. avoided being in a six-car pile-up. *(Chapter 9)*
13. Greg M. sold his company his idea. *(Chapter 13)*
14. Edna D. heard her inner guidance and saved her daughter's life. *(Chapter 12)*
15. Walt O. got the money he needed to have his house painted. *(Chapter 14)*
16. Denise N. changed from failure to success and got the job she wanted. *(Chapter 1)*
17. Jane R. received needed money, a new job, and a promotion. *(Chapter 2)*
18. Jack K. got promoted to management. *(Chapter 3)*
19. Bill K. won a $500 cash award. *(Chapter 3)*
20. Jerry and Joan B. got the money they needed to spend an entire summer in Europe. *(Chapter 5)*

21. Joe and Sheila G. saved their marriage and are happier than ever. *(Chapter 4)*
22. Rick W. got a new self-image and a new career. *(Chapter 2)*
23. Virginia G. overcame depression and nervousness during menopause. *(Chapter 6)*
24. Joseph W. overcame his secret enemies and gained a promotion at work. *(Chapter 8)*
25. Jim S. overcame the paralysis caused by a stroke. *(Chapter 7)*
26. Sarah T. overcame severe depression and developed a habit of happiness. *(Chapter 6)*
27. Virginia R. breezes through the heaviest traffic jams. *(Chapter 9)*
28. Mary J. got an urgent message to her husband that resulted in a large sales commission. *(Chapter 10)*
29. Rose A. brought eight old friends back into her life. *(Chapter 10)*
30. Robert L. protected his home so well that burglars left frustrated. *(Chapter 11)*
31. Tim R. was protected from serious injury on his job. *(Chapter 11)*
32. Robert M. broke a six-year psychotherapy habit. *(Chapter 12)*
33. Dan S. protected his home from the damage of fire. *(Chapter 11)*
34. Katherine B. reunited her family and refurnished her home. *(Chapter 15)*
35. Daren T. wrote his own happy ending to a big business deal. *(Chapter 13)*
36. Ray W. and Joan K. overcame family objections to their marriage. *(Chapter 4)*
37. Sue A. — at age 53 — found exactly the job she wanted. *(Chapter 3)*
38. George T. overcame a history of four divorces and achieved a happy marriage. *(Chapter 4)*
39. Jan W. doubled her purchasing power. *(Chapter 5)*

40. Brian B. cured his wife's depression and reunited his family. (Chapter 6)
41. Lilly D. was reunited with her sister after a two-year separation. (Chapter 10)
42. Brian N. got his salesmen to call in regularly. (Chapter 10)
43. Dottie F. protected her family from all vacation and sports accidents. (Chapter 11)
44. Don and Betty H. bought all their family's food at terrific savings. (Chapter 5)
45. Tony and Joyce D. got over a hundred dollars they weren't scheduled to receive. (Chapter 14)

Among the other case histories you will read about in the following pages is my own story. Meta-Cosmic Projection touched my life many years ago and has continually been a force in my life since that time. My life needed the invincible force of Meta-Cosmic Projection in each and every area of it. My goals, to overcome blindness, epilepsy, paralysis, and obscurity would need the unlimited power of this miraculous force if they were ever to be achieved. With the irresistible power of that miraculous force, I reached each of my goals and continue to use the secrets of Meta-Cosmic Projection in my life today. In Chapter 15 I share my story with you in detail, and I invite you to put the miraculous force of the secrets of Meta-Cosmic Projection to work in your life this very minute. These pages contain the secret Meta-Cosmic Projection techniques that will allow you to have everything you want and need. Countless thousands already know the miraculous results these secrets can bring to everyday living. Begin now to use the secrets of Meta-Cosmic Projection, and make a miracle an *everyday event* in your life!

Evelyn M. Monahan

CONTENTS

   WHAT THIS BOOK CAN DO FOR YOU 11

1 THE SECRETS OF META-COSMIC PROJECTION:
Turn on a fountain of miracles today 17

2 THE MIRACULOUS LAWS OF META-COSMIC PROJECTION 29

3 GAIN RICHES THROUGH META-COSMIC PROJECTION:
No high-paying job or rich reward is beyond your grasp 41

4 USING PSYCHIC BINOCULARS:
See your way to a happy marriage 55

5 UNLEASH A TORRENT OF RICHES AND WEALTH:
Through Meta-Cosmic Projection 69

6 EMOTIONAL CONTROL THROUGH META-COSMIC PROJECTION:
Learn to be super-cool at all times 81

7 HEALING THROUGH META-COSMIC PROJECTION:
Magic curative powers for your body 95

8 THE POWER OF META-COSMIC PROJECTION:
Tyrants and enemies cannot harm you or your loved ones 107

9 WORK WONDERS IN YOUR LIFE:
Through the secrets of Meta-Cosmic Projection 119

10 COMMUNICATE WITH OTHERS:
Through the inspiration of Meta-Cosmic Projection ... 129

11 META-COSMIC PROTECTION FOR YOU AND YOUR LOVED ONES:
At home, work and play 141

12 THE META-COSMIC DIVINING ROD:
The power that points to the answers in your life 153

13 BRING THE JOYOUS RESULTS YOU DESIRE:
Through the magic of Meta-Cosmic Projection 165

14 THE KEY TO A CONSTANT MONEY SUPPLY:
A warm security blanket through Meta-Cosmic Projection 175

15 YOUR UNLIMITED SUPPLY OF LIFETIME META-COSMIC POWER 187

1
THE SECRETS OF META-COSMIC PROJECTION:

Turn on a fountain of miracles today.

If you want to be a success in all areas of life, this book is written especially for you. You have within you a tremendous treasure known as meta-cosmic projection, and you need only to unlock the secrets of this miraculous power in order to claim your success in all things.

It is not necessary for you to hunt success as so many individuals do in today's world. You are a born success, and the secrets of meta-cosmic projection will allow you to claim that success in everything you do. Armed with the miraculous secrets of meta-cosmic projection, awaiting you in every chapter of this book, you will find that no area of life is closed to you. Whether you use the secrets of meta-cosmic projection to claim your success in business, in relationships with other people, or for monetary success, you will find that no barrier can withstand its awesome power. The secrets of meta-cosmic projection touch body, mind and spirit, and make it possible for you to claim your birthright — success in all things.

Despite the tremendous force which meta-cosmic projection puts at your command, you need not spend years learning to use it. The secrets of meta-cosmic projection are available to you this very minute. Each chapter of this book will tell you how to use meta-cosmic projection today.

If you have experienced failure in your life, it is time to change that failure to success. Through the power of meta-cosmic projection, you can transform all failure in your daily life and replace that failure with success and happiness. Once you have learned the secrets of meta-cosmic projection, success will be a habit in everything you do.

It is unfortunate that our educational system teaches students to accept supposed limitations rather than encouraging them to use the miraculous force present inside all of us. You, like most people, were probably exposed to this kind of traditional training. It is time for you to throw off this damaging training and begin to fill your life with success. No matter how elusive success may have seemed in the past, the secrets of meta-cosmic projection put success within your reach today.

One of the secrets you can use today is the secret of your psychic binoculars. With the use of psychic binoculars you can reconstruct your life this very minute. Your psychic binoculars will allow you to see clearly what you want out of life, and the power of meta-cosmic projection will allow you to reach every goal.

Denise N. Uses Psychic Binoculars to Reconstruct her Life

When I met Denise N. for the first time, she was a self-proclaimed failure. She sought me out after a talk I gave on the secrets of meta-cosmic projection. Her words left no doubt as to her attitude toward life.

"You really believe that junk, don't you?" Denise said.

I asked her why she didn't believe that she, too, could use meta-cosmic projection and why she felt it was junk.

"Are you kidding?" she said. "You can't change things with your mind. The whole world is against the average person. You have to be somebody in order to be a success in this world. I don't care what secrets you think you have, they won't work in real life."

I asked Denise what it would take to get her to change her mind. What kind of success was she after?

"That's just it," she said. "I don't even know what I want out of life. I just know that everything I ever tried turned out to be a failure. It's as if everything I wish for never works out."

"Are you willing to take a chance?" I asked. "If I can teach you a way to find out what it is you want out of life, will you at least give it a try?"

Denise shrugged her shoulders. "Why not? But I don't see how you can tell me what I want, when I don't know myself."

"I can't tell you what you want, but I can tell you how you can find out," I said. "One of the secrets of meta-cosmic projection is the use of psychic binoculars. They allow you to take a look into the future so that you can decide on a goal or any number of goals."

"Yeah, well if it's real complicated to use them, just forget it. My life is complicated enough without adding complicated techniques to it."

I assured Denise that none of the secrets of meta-cosmic projection were complicated and that she could learn to use her psychic binoculars in about fifteen minutes. She agreed to invest her time, and I began to teach her about her psychic binoculars and other secrets of meta-cosmic projection. When she left an hour later, she was still skeptical, but her attitude had changed from "It can't be done" to "I'll give it a try."

Ten days passed before I heard from Denise. She looked like a different person. Her change in attitude had softened her features and the corners of her mouth turned up instead of down.

"You're not going to believe this," she said. "I used those psychic binoculars and decided on a new job I wanted. Well, I got the job two days ago and everything looks great. Those things really work. Once I decided what I wanted, I used the other secrets you taught me, and in five days I got the job offer."

Denise had visited me, not only to let me know what happened, she wanted to know more about meta-cosmic projection. Denise is now one of the strongest advocates of psychic binoculars and the secrets of meta-cosmic projection. Her life has been changed so that success is now a habit with her.

Your Psychic Binoculars

You have within you the ability to see into your own future. Just as ordinary binoculars bring distant objects clearly into your vision, so psychic binoculars bring your future into your consciousness today. Just as ordinary binoculars make distant objects — fuzzy to the unaided eye — appear crystal clear, so your psychic binoculars will bring your wants, needs, and wishes into focus so that you can choose your goals without any second thoughts. Once you have decided what goals you want to reach, the secrets of meta-cosmic projection will put them within your reach today.

It is unfortunate that so many people wander through life unhappy with their lack of success but don't realize that they have never decided what goals they are aiming at. It is impossible for such people to experience habitual success since they have never decided what it is they want out of life.

Your psychic binoculars make it possible for you to form

a clear picture of the goals you want to reach, whether those goals are monetary, job-connected, or emotional in nature. Your psychic binoculars make it possible for you to distinguish among your wishes, your wants and your needs. Once you have made this distinction, you can set your own criteria for success and use the secrets of meta-cosmic projection to guarantee that you will reach your goals.

How to Use Your Psychic Binoculars

You will need a piece of paper and a pencil or pen to begin this exercise. Once you have the paper and pen, you need only follow these simple steps that allow you a look through your psychic binoculars to see your goals clearly.

1. Write the following two words on the piece of paper: "I wish."

2. Now close your eyes, relax, and mentally repeat the words "I wish" to yourself. Now complete that sentence with something you wish would come true. Write your wish on the paper directly after the words "I wish." For instance, if you wish for a new car, the paper would read "I wish I had a new car."

3. Again write the words "I wish" on the paper. Close your eyes and mentally repeat the words to yourself. Write your second wish on the paper.

4. For the third time write the words "I wish" on the paper. Close your eyes again and repeat the words "I wish" to yourself mentally. Write your third wish on the paper.

You are now ready for the second part of this exercise in learning to use the secrets of your psychic binoculars.

5. Write the words "I want" on the paper. Close your eyes and repeat the words "I want" to yourself mentally. Now complete the sentence and write your "want" on the piece of paper. If you want a million dollars, the paper will read "I want a million dollars."

6. Write the words "I want" once again and repeat step five. Write your second "want" on the paper.

7. For the third and final time write the words "I want" on the paper and repeat step five again.

Your paper should now contain six sentences. Three sentences that state your wishes, and three sentences that state your wants.

You are now ready for part three of this exercise in the use of your psychic binoculars.

8. Write the words "I need" on the paper, relax and repeat the words to yourself mentally. Again write your completed sentence on the paper. If you feel you need a new job, the paper will read "I need a new job."

9. Now write the words "I need" again, and once again, relax and repeat the words to yourself. Write your second need on the paper.

10. For the third and final time, write the words "I need" on the paper and repeat step eight. Write your third need on the paper.

You are now ready to take an even closer look through your psychic binoculars. Read over the nine sentences you have written. Are your wishes, wants, and needs the same, or are they different? Is a wish the same as a want? Is a want the same as a need? Relax for a moment, close your eyes and ask yourself what a *wish* is, what a *want* is, and what a *need* is?

The fact is that a wish, a want, and a need are different things, even though a person can need, want, and wish for the same thing.

It is important that you recognize this difference so that you don't spend your life seeking goals that really have no meaning for you.

A wish can be defined in different ways, but one thing always true of wishes is the fact that they are not packed with energy that moves a person to action. Look through my psychic binoculars with me for a moment. For a long time I *wished* I could play the piano. Today, many years later, I still can't play the piano. My psychic binoculars allowed me to see why I never learned to be the pianist I wished to be. My trouble was that I only *wished* to play the piano, but I never really wanted to learn. I failed to put any energy and action behind my wish. Wishes are like that. They most often remain thoughts that people do nothing to bring into reality.

If I had really wanted to play the piano, the story would be different. I would have backed up my *want* with energy for action, and sought and taken advantage of all opportunities to take piano lessons. I never really *wanted* to learn to play the piano and so I am still unable to play the piano today. Sometimes I still think — "Gee, I wish I could play the piano." — but with my psychic binoculars I can see that my thought is still a wish I'm not ready to put my energy into.

Are your wishes like my wish to play the piano? Are you willing to back them with action? If you are ready to do something to bring your wish into actuality, your *wish* may really be a *want*.

Wants, like wishes, may have several definitions, but, like wishes, all wants have something in common. Wants are backed by action. Again look through my psychic binoculars with me. A few years ago, I decided that I wanted to earn a masters degree and a doctorate in the field of psychology. Because this was a *want* and not merely a *wish*, I took the necessary steps to enroll in graduate school. Because I truly wanted those degrees, I took the necessary courses, did the required research, and wrote the necessary dissertation to fulfill the requirements for both degrees. I have earned both a masters and a doctorate in the field of psychology, because I wanted them instead of merely wishing for them. *Wants* are desires you are willing to *invest your time and energy in*, in order to reach your goal. When you truly want something, you will seek and take advantage of opportunities that will help you reach your wanted goal.

Are you willing to invest your time and energy in order to reach the goals you say you want? If you are not willing to back your wants with energy for action, perhaps they are not truly goals you want to reach. If you are not ready to seek and take advantage of opportunities that lead to the goals you want, perhaps your *wants* are really meaningless wishes. Goals you really only intend to dream about reaching without any action on your part, are *wishes* and not truly *wanted* goals.

Read the three sentences in which you stated your wants. Now relax, close your eyes, and mentally repeat the wants you have listed. Look into yourself and decide if the goals you have stated are truly things you want.

Human beings have many needs in common and many needs that are unique to individuals. Needs are frequently confused with wants, but do not necessarily have anything to do with what a person wants. Denise N. was able to see this difference by using her psychic binoculars. Denise first stated that she needed a million dollars. When she took a closer look through her psychic binoculars, Denise discovered that she didn't really *need* a million dollars at all. Any debts which Denise had did not come close to a million dollars. She did not *need* a million dollars to get her out of debt or to pay for a needed surgical operation. She did not *need* a million dollars to be herself. In fact, she did not need a million dollars at all.

If you have a true *need* to reach a goal, then you need that goal to be everything you can be. If you truly need something in your life, then without that something, you cannot truly be yourself. A *need* for a million dollars could only be a true need if a person had a million dollars worth of debts or actually could not reach a certain goal without a million dollars.

An example of real *needs* which all human beings have in common is the need to be loved and accepted and the need to love and accept. The needs for food, safety, and shelter are also shared by human beings. Human beings do not have a great number of actual *needs* but they often confuse their needs with their wants and wishes. Read the three sentences in which you listed your needs. Relax, close your eyes, and repeat these listed needs to yourself mentally. With the aid of your psychic binoculars, look closely at these *needs* and decide if they are real *needs* or more accurately *wants* or even *wishes*.

It is unfortunate that most human beings never discover their psychic binoculars. Such people go through life *wishing* for things they don't really want or need, and *needing* things they neither want nor wish to attain.

Your psychic binoculars allow you to see your goals in the proper perspective. You can decide what you really *need* to be happy and successful, and what you *want* that will help you to be happy and successful. Your psychic binoculars allow you to stop wasting time *wishing* for things you neither *want* nor *need*. With your goals clearly set, you can use the secrets of meta-cosmic projection to attain each and every one of them.

Since you now know the difference between wishes, wants, and needs, you should repeat steps one through ten. Chances are your list of nine sentences will change considerably. Take time now to look through your psychic binoculars and complete steps one through ten again.

How have your listed goals changed? Did you discover that some of the things you thought you wanted were only things you wished to have or do? Did you discover that some of the things you thought you needed were simply things you wanted or wished to possess?

Now that you have a clearer picture of your real goals in life, of the things you really *want* and *need,* you can begin to use the powerful secrets of meta-cosmic projection to reach your goals. With the powerful secrets that await you in the following chapters, no true goal is impossible for you to reach. The secrets of meta-cosmic projection put success in all things within your reach today. Now that you have found your goals through the use of your psychic binoculars, it is time for you to claim the success you have always deserved. *The Secrets of Meta-Cosmic Projection* give you the power to make success a habit in your everyday life.

You will learn to use the impenetrable force of your Meta-Cosmic Shield technique, the irresistible power of your Psychic Organizer technique, the incredible force of your Meta-Cosmic Projection Telephone technique, and your always answered Meta-Cosmic Prayer. These secrets are at your fingertips this very moment. Put them to work in your life today.

2

THE MIRACULOUS LAWS OF META-COSMIC PROJECTION

The miraculous laws of meta-cosmic projection have created the very world in which you live. Everything you see before you was once only a thought. It was the miraculous laws of meta-cosmic projection that turned those thoughts into material forms. These miraculous secret laws touch past, present, and future and can be controlled by you.

Your thoughts have already created the world in which you live and interact. If failure has touched your life in any way, the miraculous laws of meta-cosmic projection can turn that failure to success and make success a habit in all areas of your life.

If you have wandered through life until now without knowing what you really wanted and needed to be happy and successful, it is no wonder that your life has been confused and untouched by success. Without setting goals for yourself, you can never know true happiness, and your life is bound to be marked by confusion and failure.

The laws of meta-cosmic projection never stand still. These miraculous laws have been in force in your life from the moment of your birth. In order to make these laws work for you, it is necessary that you learn the secrets of meta-cosmic projection — the very secrets that are presented to you in this book.

When I say that the laws of meta-cosmic projection have created the world in which you live today, I do not mean that you have used the laws to your benefit. In the past, and, in fact, to this very place in time, you have had certain ideas about yourself, your family, your friends, your job, and many other areas of life. Those ideas were expressed in your thoughts. You have thought about yourself in a certain way and have expected certain events to take place in your world. The image you have had of yourself has determined, to a large extent, the manner in which people have responded to you. If you have thought of yourself as a person who can't do anything right, most likely others have seen you as a failure. If your image of yourself has been one in which you consider yourself unattractive and dull, most likely, people have responded to you as if you were an undesirable bore. The laws of meta-cosmic projection are constantly at work creating your world from the substance of your thoughts.

The technique presented to you in this book will allow you to use the laws of meta-cosmic projection to create the world you want. The secrets of meta-cosmic projection will allow you to set aside the old image you have had of yourself and your abilities, and replace that image with one of success and happiness. The miraculous power of meta-cosmic projection works with the speed of light and is at your finger tips this very moment. No matter how hopeless a situation seems to you, the secrets of meta-cosmic projection can change it to one in which success is a natural conclusion.

Meta-Cosmic Projection Conquers a Hopeless Situation

When I first met Rick W., he had one of the poorest, if not *the* poorest, self-image and success-image of anyone I had ever met. He was convinced that he was completely helpless concerning his own success or failure. Rick saw himself as an inadequate person who had nothing to offer to a company, to a conversation, to another person, or to himself. For twenty years Rick had wandered through life not daring to seek or even hope for success. In his own mind he was a born failure. He had flunked out of his freshman year in college. In two years' time he had held and been fired from four different jobs.

Rick quickly told me that seeking my help was a last resort. "I just don't know anywhere else to turn," said Rick. "I really don't think *you* can change my life either. In fact, I think I'm just a born loser."

"You're right about one thing, I can't change your life," I said. "I can teach you how to change it though."

Rick looked just as skeptical as when he first introduced himself.

"What are you going to do, give me a magic formula?" he asked. "I'd better tell you that I don't believe in magic."

"That's fine," I said. "I have no special magic to teach you. I do have a few secrets, though, that can turn you and your life around. The magic, however, is all within you. What I'd like to do is teach you how to use the secrets of meta-cosmic projection, if you want to learn to make success a habit."

"I don't mind trying anything, but if meta-cosmic projection works, it will be the first time something has been successful for me."

"What is your idea of success, Rick? What would it take to make you consider yourself and your life successful?" I asked.

Rick looked puzzled and shook his head. "I don't even know. I don't know what I want. I'm just tired of constant failure," Rick said.

For forty minutes I talked with Rick about psychic binoculars and the secret laws of meta-cosmic projection. Slowly, very slowly, the total skepticism began to leave Rick's face.

"It sounds logical, but are you sure it will work?" Rick asked.

"If you use the techniques I've just taught you, it can't help but work. There is no such thing as failure once you know how to use meta-cosmic projection," I said.

Rick decided he'd give meta-cosmic projection a try. In five days I received a call from him.

"I've got a job interview tomorrow. It's for a job I really want. I used the secrets of meta-cosmic projection to decide what I wanted and to get the interview. Now I'm scared I won't get the job," Rick said.

We spent thirty minutes on the phone. I explained, once again, that there is nothing stronger than meta-cosmic projection. When we hung up the phone, Rick was determined to use the secrets of meta-cosmic projection to get the job and keep it.

An entire week passed before I heard from Rick again. To my surprise, he was calling during his lunch hour.

"The interview was a breeze. They hired me on the spot," Rick said happily. "The job is really interesting and the company is going to pay my college tuition. Naturally, I'll have to go to night school, but now that I know what I want I won't have any trouble. These secrets of meta-cosmic projection have really changed my whole life. After all this time, I'm finally a winner."

Rick has been with that company for more than a year and has already received two promotions. He has maintained a "B" average in his night classes in college, and is thinking about going for an MBA once he has finished his undergraduate work. The secrets of meta-cosmic projection have unlocked a world of success for Rick. It will do the same for you.

Your Meta-Cosmic Technique for Unlocking the Winner Within Yourself

There are many wonderful things about meta-cosmic projection, but the secret you are about to learn is one of the best. The secret is this — you don't have to have all your goals figured out in order to unlock the winner inside yourself. You can begin to enjoy success in your life once you have decided that success is what you want.

The following step-by-step technique has brought success into the lives of countless numbers of people, and it will do the same for you. It should be used after you have looked through your psychic binoculars and decided what success is as far as you are concerned.

1. Sit in a comfortable chair and allow your muscles to relax completely.

2. Close your eyes and form a clear picture of yourself in your mind. See yourself as you want to be. For example, if you want to be a more assertive person, see yourself speaking up in a situation in which you previously found it difficult to express yourself.

3. Now change the focus of your consciousness and see yourself being congratulated by your friends, family, and associates for being a person committed to his own growth. For example, you might see yourself in your living room surrounded by people you know, and carrying on a conversation similar to the following one.

Person I "I really want to congratulate you. You have really made strides in your own personal growth."

> *Person II* "You have my congratulations too. You really have changed a lot. There doesn't seem to be anything you can't do well."
>
> *Person III* "I'll second that! I don't know what you've done to yourself, but you've turned into a real winner. I can't imagine you as anything but successful."
>
> *Person IV* "Successful is right! Everything you get into turns into an instant success."
>
> *You* "Thank you for your compliments. I have to admit that I do like the feeling of being so completely successful."

The number of people you include in this exercise is up to you. You decide who you will include, what they will say, and how you will respond. It is advisable, however, not to people your meta-cosmic projection with more than four persons, not including yourself.

This exercise should be used twice a day in order to keep the winner in yourself unlocked and active in your life.

Begin to use this meta-cosmic projection technique today. It holds a powerful secret that will bring success as easy as one, two, three!

You Are More Powerful Than You Think

Most people have no real idea of the power they possess within their own minds. The miracle of meta-cosmic projection can make that unlimited power available to you today. You need only make use of the secrets of meta-cosmic projection in order to find the well-spring of your true strength. If you have ever felt yourself to be at someone else's mercy, and didn't like the feeling, the secrets of meta-cosmic projection can give you the upper hand in every situation.

Once you have learned to use these secrets, no one on earth is more powerful than you!

Jane R. Found Her Power to Attract Money in a Hurry

Jane R. was introduced to me by a former student. At the time of our meeting, Jane was in a state of intense anxiety concerning her financial situation. Four months earlier Jane had moved to Atlanta in hopes of finding a job and making her home in this growing city. She had three job interviews during her first two weeks in Atlanta and one interview seemed very promising. Jane was to hear from the company in a day or two and fully expected to be offered the job.

The evening of the day of Jane's promising interview she slipped and fell down a flight of stairs in her town house apartment, breaking two bones in her left leg. She was hospitalized for three days while the leg was set and placed in a cast.

As Jane had expected, she was offered the job she wanted so badly. When the interviewer learned that Jane had broken her leg and would be in a cast for approximately eight weeks, he expressed his regrets that they could not hold the opening. The job was given to another applicant and Jane was left to recuperate and job hunt again, once her leg had mended.

The period of recuperation was marked by two other setbacks. First, Jane contracted a moderately serious case of pneumonia that saw her hospitalized again, this time for one week. Following her return from the hospital, Jane developed an ear infection that required several visits to a specialist and expensive medication to clear it up. (Jane had no knowledge of the miracle of metaphysical healing!)

Three unexpected emergencies had all but depleted the savings Jane had planned to use as a cushion until she had a job and a regular paycheck.

"I have about forty dollars left in my checking account and that's nowhere near enough to pay last month's rent, let alone the rent for this month," said Jane. "If I had had insurance I wouldn't be in this fix. Now I'm faced with having to move from an apartment I can no longer afford. I know I can move in with Judy for a while, but I'd have to store my furniture and I can't even afford that." She paused. "Besides the inconvenience of moving, I hate to damage my credit by leaving the apartment rent unpaid."

Jane had certainly seen her share of problems since her arrival in Atlanta, and felt the future looked pretty bleak. Her leg was out of the cast, but she had not received a job offer in the two weeks she had been able to seek employment again.

"I talked to two banks about a loan," she said. "I'm afraid, however, that without a job, both turned me down flat. In fact, they told me no one was likely to grant me a loan without a job or collateral."

Jane was at the point of tears. Her voice was shaky as she said, "I'm at my wits-end. I'm willing to try anything, including this meta-cosmic projection that Judy told me about. It sounds weird to me, but I have absolutely nothing to lose. What I need fast is money for last month's and this month's rent. I feel certain I can get a job, but it may take another month."

For an hour we talked about the secrets of meta-cosmic projection. Jane needed money in a hurry, so we concentrated on a technique that would bring her the loan she wanted. That afternoon and evening Jane was to use meta-cosmic projection, seeing herself being granted a loan by a bank. She was to use the same technique in the morning just before applying to a third bank for a signature loan.

"I hope you know what you're talking about," Jane said. "A signature loan to an individual without collateral or a job would be most unusual."

I borrowed from an Air Force quotation and said, "The unusual, meta-cosmic projection does right away — the impossible takes a little longer."

At seven p.m. the next night I received a phone call from

Jane. "You're not going to believe this," she said. "I got the loan, enough to handle the rent and groceries."

"Terrific, Jane," I responded.

"You haven't heard the best part yet," she said. "The loan officer asked me what kind of work I was looking for and it just so happened that the bank has an opening. I have an interview with their personnel office in the morning. I'll let you know how it comes out."

"Use your meta-cosmic projection technique tonight and before your interview, and it will come out fine," I said.

"You mean it will work for jobs too!" said Jane.

"Meta-cosmic projection will work on anything you really want," I said.

Jane phoned the following afternoon. "Three cheers for meta-cosmic projection!" she began. "I am now among the employed. I start work tomorrow."

"That's great, Jane," I said. "I'm really happy for you. Give me a call sometime and let me know how you're doing."

"You can count on that," said Jane. "With this meta-cosmic projection thing, I can already tell you that everything will be A-Okay." She paused for a second, then said, "The next call you receive will be from my apartment instead of a phone booth. I can now afford a telephone."

Four months later, I was pleasantly surprised by a visit from Jane R.

"I just had to come by to let you know I got a promotion. I used meta-cosmic projection to bring it about. You know, the more you use these secrets the better they work."

"You've discovered one of the secrets of meta-cosmic projection," I said.

"That's not the only one I've discovered," said Jane. "My social life has really taken shape. Everything I do is lots more enjoyable. There just isn't anything the secrets of meta-cosmic projection can't handle."

You Can Profit from Jane's Success

The same secrets of meta-cosmic projection that worked for Jane are at your command today. No one has to be a genius to use them, although I am sure that they will work the same miracles in the life of a genius as they have so often worked in my life and the lives of countless numbers of people.

In the following chapters you will learn specific secrets of meta-cosmic projection to be used in specific situations. Their unlimited power is at your command at this very moment. It is time that you tap your own unlimited source of endless power by making the secrets of meta-cosmic projection a force in your daily life.

3

GAIN RICHES THROUGH META-COSMIC PROJECTION:

No high-paying job or rich reward is beyond your grasp.

It is a sad truth that many people today work at jobs they don't like. Even people who like their jobs often do not like their working conditions. Workers in offices and factories find themselves involved in personality clashes or immersed in details that dull a job they might otherwise find interesting.

If you have ever thought that you would like a different job or that your working conditions could certainly be improved, you can now turn your thoughts into reality. The secrets of meta-cosmic projection give you the power to obtain the job you want, and to create the working conditions that will allow you to enjoy your work. You need never spend another day at a job you hate or work another hour in a job situation that makes your working hours miserable. Through the secrets of meta-cosmic projection your job can be a snap.

You have already been given some of the secrets of your psychic binoculars. Those secrets are your key to deciding just what job you want, and what working conditions will make that job more enjoyable for you. You need only look through your psychic binoculars and see what it is you want in a job. Use pencil and paper and write down, "The job I want . . ." Now take a deep breath, close your eyes, and listen to the sound of your own higher consciousness. Once you have heard your own thoughts, write them down, completing the sentence you have begun. Your sentence might be completed and read "The job I want will allow me to work out of doors."

Once you have completed the first sentence, look through your psychic binoculars again and write the beginning of the second sentence "The job I want..." Again take a deep breath, close your eyes, and listen to your own higher consciousness. Write the completion of the second sentence. For example, your second sentence might read "The job I want will allow me a great deal of freedom."

Now look through your psychic binoculars again and write the beginning of the third sentence "The job I want..." Again take a deep breath, close your eyes, and listen. Write the completion of your third sentence. For example, "The job I want will allow me to be creative."

Your psychic binoculars have now allowed you to see what it is you want in a job. This is extremely important, since one can never reach a goal unless he knows what that goal is for him. If a person never sees his goal clearly, how is he to attain it? More than likely, a person without a goal wanders through the job market never finding the job he wants, since he has never decided what he does want in a job. With the secrets of your psychic binoculars and the miraculous power of meta-cosmic projection, you can choose and get the job you want.

Your psychic binoculars can also allow you to see the working conditions you want in your job. Your working conditions are very important since even the most interesting job can become distasteful if the conditions surrounding it are unpleasant. You can decide on the working conditions you want by using your psychic binoculars.

Once again, you will need paper and pencil. Write the beginning of the sentence you will complete with the help of your psychic binoculars. "The working conditions I want..." Now take a deep breath, close your eyes, and listen to your own higher consciousness. Once you have heard your high self, write your thought completing the first sentence. For example, "The working conditions I want will put me in contact with people I like and who like me."

Now write the beginning of the second sentence. "The working conditions I want..." Again take a deep breath and close your eyes. Your psychic binoculars will allow you to see into your higher consciousness and hear the voice of your high self. Write the completion of the second sentence. For example, "The working conditions I want will allow my talents to be used and recognized."

Repeat the same process for your third and final sentence.

You now have before you six sentences that state what you want in clear and unmistakable language. Once your goals are definitely defined in this way, you can use the secrets of meta-cosmic projection to attain each and every one of them.

Why Not Receive a Promotion?

Job advancement is important to most people. For Jack K. it was extremely important. Jack had taken a job with a large company without giving much thought as to where he wanted that job to lead. After two years in the same job classification, Jack became generally unhappy at work. He was unable to say what was causing his unhappiness with his job, or why his feelings concerning his work had changed. Jack's unhappiness at work began to spill over into his home life. Still Jack could not put his finger on the reasons for his dissatisfaction at work.

When his own feelings became very uncomfortable, Jack mentioned them to a family friend. That friend introduced Jack to me.

In spite of the fact that Jack's dissatisfaction at work was a mystery to him, it was a condition I had seen many times. I explained to Jack the importance of deciding what it was he wanted from a job and the working conditions he wanted to surround his work. He listened attentively as I told him about his psychic binoculars and the secrets of meta-cosmic projection. Before he left my presence, he used his psychic binoculars and discovered what it was he wanted in connection with his job and working conditions.

"This is unbelievable," Jack said. "I had no idea I wanted a promotion so badly. Now I realize that I have been feeling cheated and 'looked over' because I haven't been promoted into a management job."

Jack left with a firm resolve to get the promotion to management which he now realized he wanted. His psychic binoculars had allowed him to see things he was overlooking with his ordinary eyesight.

Two weeks passed before I heard from Jack again. His voice bounced out of the telephone receiver.

"I got my promotion. I have been a department manager for three whole days. Things are really going great. Work is interesting again and my family says I'm a different person at home. No more sad sack! I am really happy again."

I congratulated Jack on his promotion and shared the excitement of his happiness. He used the secrets of meta-cosmic projection to attain the exact promotion he wanted. Jack had learned more than one valuable secret. He now knew that it was foolish to be unhappy at work when, with the use of his psychic binoculars, he could discover exactly what it would take to make him happy with his job. He also knew that with the secrets of meta-cosmic projection, he could attain the goals he needed to make him happy with his job and work conditions.

"I wish I had known about meta-cosmic projection years ago," said Jack. "Now that I do know its secrets, and how to use my psychic binoculars, I'll never spend another unhappy day at work or anywhere else."

Why Not a New Job?

If what you want is an entirely new job, or if you are unemployed and seeking employment, the secrets of meta-cosmic projection are your key to a new future. The miraculous secrets of your psychic binoculars and the unlimited force of meta-cosmic projection will allow you to obtain the exact job opening you want. There is no need for you to hunt furiously day in and day out hoping to "luck up" upon a job opening. The secrets of meta-cosmic projection can have that job opening waiting for you.

New Job Changed a Woman's Life

Sue A. had what many people might consider a very ordinary life. She kept house and raised three children after her husband's death. Her husband had provided enough money in insurance and investments to maintain his young family until all of the children were in college. It was at this time, when all three children were away from home, when Sue A. decided she wanted a job. Sue was fifty-three years old and had no particular skills to offer the business world. She had never had a regular job, and she didn't type or take shorthand.

For two months Sue beat the pavement from office to office answering ads that said "Will train." Unfortunately, as far as Sue was concerned, no one wanted to hire and train her.

When I met Sue her self-image had suffered a damaging blow. She had begun to see herself as a person who could do nothing that would allow her to earn a gainful and respectable living. Doubts about her own self-worth had begun to make their way into her daily thinking.

"What I'd really like to do is work in a combination nursery-kindergarten," said Sue. "The only problem there is that people want someone with nursery experience or a degree in child development or education." She paused briefly and said, "Now I may not have a degree or actual kindergarten experience, but I've raised three children of my own and looked after many a neighbor's child in the past. I just know I could do the work if I had the chance."

Sue was extremely attentive as I explained the secrets of meta-cosmic projection to her. She listened without distraction to information about her psychic binoculars.

"I'm sure about the kind of work I want," she said. "The only problem is I've been to every nursery-kindergarten in the entire area and not one wanted to hire me."

I asked if there was any particular kindergarten at which she wanted to work, and when she answered, yes, I suggested that she use the secrets of meta-cosmic projection to get a job with them.

"They've turned me down three times," Sue said. "It seems all their staff has at least two years of college." Sue shrugged her shoulders and smiled. "What the devil! I might as well try for the one I really want. What do I have to lose?"

For two weeks Sue used meta-cosmic projection aimed at getting her a job at the kindergarten of her choice. In the middle of the third week I received a call from her.

"I start work with them tomorrow. They don't even want me to wait until Monday," Sue said. "I spent this afternoon talking to the director and he hired me before I left."

Sue was really excited and her voice was electric with enthusiasm.

"They called me on the phone this morning and asked me to drop by about one o'clock to discuss a possible job opening." Sue paused only long enough to catch her breath. "I was ten minutes early and after talking for almost three hours, they hired me. I'm the only person they have ever hired without a college background — that meta-cosmic projection really works."

The secrets of meta-cosmic projection had indeed worked for Sue A., just as they have worked for countless others, and just as they will work for you. Sue's entire life was changed from one in which she had little purpose, to a life filled with sharing, excitement and meaning. For Sue it was not the need for money that led her to seek a job, but a need for purpose and human contact. The secrets of meta-cosmic projection work without fail no matter what reason you have for wanting a job. Begin to put these secrets to work in your life today.

Personality Clashes Are No Match for Meta-Cosmic Projection

Many times problems concerning a person's job do not spring from the job itself, but from friction between two or more co-workers. Most often these personality clashes are based on feelings rather than logical thinking. This feeling base often makes these clashes more difficult to handle by ordinary means than actual specific job problems.

Bob L. is one young man who turned to meta-cosmic projection to resolve a personality clash at work. Bob had no complaints concerning the actual duties of his job. In fact, he liked his work immensely. The one problem for which there seemed no solution was Bob's relationship with his co-worker, Roy W. Roy had taken an immediate dislike to Bob from the day Bob entered Roy's department. Since Roy was Bob's immediate supervisor, the situation often grew touchy where Bob's job evaluations were concerned. Roy constantly saw Bob as a "show off" and a "big mouth." On several occasions Roy's reports had put an end to possible promotions for Bob.

"I just don't know what else to do," said Bob. "Every time I present a new idea that will increase the efficiency of the shipping department, Roy overlooks my suggestions and sees me as a big mouthed show off." The frustration in Bob's face and voice could not be overlooked. "A month after I made a certain suggestion, the idea was introduced as Roy's brain child. He got all the credit for the time and money it saved. On top of that, he got furious with me for trying to point out that I had suggested the very same thing a month earlier."

No doubt about it — Bob L. was in a ticklish situation. No situation, however, is too tough or too delicate for the secrets of meta-cosmic projection. After a long discussion, Bob determined to use meta-cosmic projection to put an end to the personality problem between Roy and him.

An entire month passed before I heard from Bob. "I'd like to invite you to my home for dinner," Bob said happily. "Roy W and his wife will be there and I think you deserve to see the results of that technique. Would you believe that we are now on the same bowling team at work. In fact, Roy just recommended me for a raise on merit alone."

I didn't have to go to Bob's home for dinner to know that his personality clash with Roy W. was a thing of the past. The secrets of meta-cosmic prejection had resolved it completely. "Cold war enemies" had become warmhearted teammates and friends.

Meta-Cosmic Projection Solves Problems and Brings Cash Award

Bill K's story was told to me only after he had used meta-cosmic projection to his complete satisfaction. Bill introduced himself over the telephone early one Saturday morning. He told me that he had been introduced to meta-cosmic projection by a friend who had learned the technique from me almost a year earlier.

"I just thought you'd like to know how well meta-cosmic projection worked for me," said Bill.

Bill went on to explain that the plant where he worked had been bothered for years with a problem in their shipping department that seemed to have no solution.

"Top management worked on the problem for years, but nothing they came up with seemed to do any good," Bill said. "When the company offered a cash award of $500 to anyone who could present a workable solution, I began to think seriously about the thing."

Bill went on to say that he hadn't come up with a workable solution even after he had given it serious thought for three weeks. He mentioned the problem and the cash award to a friend who quickly told him about meta-cosmic projection and taught him how to use it.

"In one week I came up with a solution I just knew would work. I wrote it up and submitted it to my foreman. A week later, they were trying it out in the shipping department." Bill paused only for a second. "Well, after three weeks, they knew their problem was solved. I received my $500 award just yesterday. I just had to let you know how I feel about meta-cosmic projection. It's terrific!"

I thanked Bill for letting me know about his experience with meta-cosmic projection, and congratulated him on the receipt of his cash award. It's always nice to know that someone is thoughtful enough to fill me in on his success.

Psychic Binoculars and Meta-Cosmic Projection Can Create Better Working Conditions

For many years psychologists have been aware that the working conditions which surround an individual at his job have an immense influence on the worker's productivity and morale. Sherry D. became acutely aware of this fact when she was transferred by her firm to a branch office in a small town. The branch office occupied an old building and the interior of individual offices in the building left much to be desired. Everything was painted a drab institutional green. There were no pictures on the walls and the blinds on the windows were broken, dusty and did nothing more than keep out sunlight.

In addition to being appalled by the drab conditions existing in the entire office, Sherry was depressed by the thought of spending close to 40 hours a week in a dark, drab, uncomfortable office. For a year Sherry had used meta-cosmic projection, but was not too sure how it should be put to use to better her working conditions.

"I guess part of my problem is that I don't know where to begin," said Sherry. "Everything in that office is such a mess. No one but me seems interested in improving conditions. According to the office manager, there isn't any money for physical improvements." Sherry shook her head in frustration. "I just don't seem to be able to get across the fact that those physical conditions affect morale. Like I said, I don't even know where to begin."

We talked for about an hour concerning psychic binoculars and meta-cosmic projection. In her frustration and, as Sherry later admitted, her anger, she had completely forgotten about the power of her psychic binoculars. Once Sherry was reminded that she could use her psychic binoculars in order to find the best place to begin to get her office redecorated, she was determined to begin immediately. She used her psychic binoculars to set her goals for her office and began to use meta-cosmic projection right away.

Six weeks passed before I heard from Sherry again. Her voice bubbled from the telephone.

"This won't come as a surprise to you, but my office is

now a thing of beauty," said Sherry. "The home office suddenly decided to spruce up all their branch offices. They started with ours since it was the most in need of a face lift."

Sherry went on to talk about the color combinations, new carpets, drapes in place of old blinds, new furniture, and pictures on the walls.

"The morale here sure has improved," she said. "Even the office manager admits it's a great improvement." She laughed lightly and said. "I've just begun to talk with him about meta-cosmic projection and he's already anxious to use it in his life. He has a house he and his wife want to remodel. If it turns out half as good as our office, it will look great."

Your Secret Meta-Cosmic Projection Technique to Obtain Your Dream Job

1. Use your psychic binoculars to determine exactly what you want in a job.

2. Sit in a relaxed position, close your eyes, and give your attention to your breathing. Make no attempt to control your breathing, but keep it in your awareness for one minute.

3. Form a motion picture in your mind seeing yourself being offered your dream job. Hear, in your mind, the job offer being extended to you.

4. Now see and hear the benefits and salary you want offered to you. Be very specific concerning your salary and working hours. For example, if you want a salary of $10,000 a year and you want your hours to be from 9 a.m. to 5 p.m., see and hear the person offering the job saying, "Your salary will start at $10,000 a year and your hours will be from 9 a.m. to 5 p.m."

5. Now in your mind see and hear yourself accepting the job offer.

6. In your mind see and hear the person who offers the job state your starting date.

7. See and hear yourself agree to the starting date.

8. Now in your mind see and hear yourself at work in your new job. See and hear yourself performing the duties of that job.

9. Finally, see yourself being congratulated for performing the job well. Hear the words of congratulations spoken to you.

10. Relax and allow your mind to remain open to silence. Again, for sixty seconds, put your attention on your breathing. Now go about the regular activities of your day.

Repeat this technique three times a day.

With the secrets of meta-cosmic projection, you can have the job you want, the working conditions you want, the salary you want, and the hours you want. You need only use the secret techniques given to you here. Follow it faithfully and you cannot fail.

With the miraculous secrets of meta-cosmic projection, you are your own boss.

4

USING PSYCHIC BINOCULARS:

See your way to a happy marriage.

Rarely does a day pass but that a story of a tragedy having its roots in marital problems is not carried in the news media. The institution of marriage is seen by sociologists, psychologists and people in general as facing many crises. The divorce rate in our country has soared the last ten years, and many people are speaking in favor of alternative styles of marriage. The "open marriage" has been discussed in books and newspapers and on radio and television.

Perhaps what the institution of marriage needs is not alternative styles (which range from "open marriage" where both partners are free to engage in sexual acts with people other than their spouses, to "multiple marriage" where four, five, or more people consider themselves married all to each other), but an alternative way for people to solve problems that arise in conventional marriage as we have known it for centuries. Rather than seeking new *forms* of "marriage" which can be equated to revolution, perhaps we would do better to seek new methods of dealing with marital problems more effectively. The secrets of meta-cosmic projection can provide the means of solving marital problems, and strengthening the bonds between husband and wife. Those powerful secrets are available to you this very minute. In this chapter the secrets of meta-cosmic projection are presented that can restore new life to marriages, solve the problems separating husband from wife from family, establish happy, strong marriages, and allow people to enjoy the closeness and happiness offered through union in marriage.

Marriage Saved with Meta-Cosmic Projection

Joe and Sheila G. had been married for seven years when they sought my help. Both of them told much the same story. The first four years of their marriage, they had been extremely happy. In the fifth year of marriage, they began to feel estranged, and in the sixth and seventh years that estrangement had created a large gulf between them. They were giving serious consideration to divorce but felt that, if at all possible, they would prefer to save their marriage.

"Don't get me wrong," said Sheila. "Neither of us wants an empty shell of a marriage. If there is a way, however, to get back the feelings and closeness we had in the first four years of our marriage, we want to know about it."

"I feel the same way," said Joe. "We were really happy those first four years, then..." He paused briefly. "Then... well, something happened. I don't know what it was that caused it, but we both seemed to pull back. We communicated less and less and drifted further and further apart."

Neither could say exactly what it was that brought about the change in their marital life, but both agreed that the change had also affected every facet of their lives.

Sheila and Joe had heard about psychic binoculars and meta-cosmic projection through a friend. Now their request was clear.

"Teach us to use meta-cosmic projection so that we can save our marriage," said Sheila.

I explained to them that it was extremely important for them to decide what it was they wanted from their marriage. They could use their psychic binoculars to discover the things they wanted and needed from their relationship. Both readily agreed and set about individually using their psychic binoculars to get a clear view of what they wanted their marriage to provide. When they had done this and had a list of their "wants" and "needs" regarding marriage, we spent some time sharing the information each had gained. During an hour discussion, Sheila and Joe learned more about their individual wants and needs and gained a clearer understanding of each other's wants and needs. Together they decided on their goals for a rejuvenated marriage. They left determined to achieve those goals, in order to bring new happiness to their marriage and save it from divorce.

Approximately seven weeks passed before I heard from either Joe or Sheila. Then one afternoon my phone rang and Sheila asked when they might stop by to talk with me. We set a time for the next day and the couple arrived right on time. Without either of them referring to their marriage, I could immediately see an absence of the tensions present at the time of their first visit.

"We wanted you to know that things have been going great since we started using meta-cosmic projection," said Joe. He smiled broadly. "That stuff really works. We've been like newlyweds for the past five weeks."

Sheila smiled and said, "Not quite. We're much happier than we were as newlyweds. We know what we both want and need from our marriage, and with meta-cosmic projection, we've attained our goals." She smiled at her husband and turned again to me. "We decided to have a baby, and what's great about it is that we don't want the baby to save our marriage, we want a baby because our marriage is so good, we want a family."

We talked for an hour or so and Sheila and Joe left arm in arm, thanking me for introducing them to meta-cosmic projection.

This young couple is not unique. They experienced many of the problems that plague marriages today. With the secrets of meta-cosmic projection they overcame the problems which threatened their marriage and brought new happiness and meaning to their relationship. They followed in the path of countless others before them who used meta-cosmic projection to save their marriages and bring new happiness to their relationships. That same path is open to you, and the steps needed to follow it can be found in this chapter.

Meta-Cosmic Projection Makes Marriage Possible

Frequently problems spring up between a couple even before their marriage takes place. This was the case with Ray W. and Joan K. Ray was an only child, and his parents had invested many of their unfulfilled aspirations in him. They had his life pretty well mapped out before Ray was five years old. In their plan Ray would attend certain schools, take music lessons, engage in certain sports (and be a letter man in each), have a certain "class" of friends, and marry a "suitable" mate sometime in his twenty-eighth year.

Things went pretty well for Ray's parents until his senior year in college. He had lived out their plans for him, and the future, as they saw it, looked terrific. Then Ray announced that, following his graduation, he intended to marry a young woman he had been dating for the past seven months. His parents were stunned. Ray was six years short of his schedule for marriage. Besides, the young lady, Joan K., didn't seem to Mr. and Mrs. W. to be a suitable mate for their son.

Immediately they launched a campaign to "bring Ray to his senses" and break up his relationship with Joan. Letters and phone calls from his parents besieged Ray almost daily. They listed every possible objection to their son's marriage that imagination could possibly conceive. When this tactic did not get the desired effect, they seemed to weaken and asked Ray to bring Joan to meet them for dinner at their home.

After an exchange of pleasantries, Mr. and Mrs. W. appealed to Joan to be "sensible" and call off her engagement to their son. Joan was polite but insistent that she and Ray loved each other and would be married as planned. Ray and Joan left the house when it became clear that an attack upon Joan was the only reason for which an invitation to dinner had been extended.

Two days later Ray received a call from his father telling him that Ray's mother had suffered "a slight heart attack" and had been confined to her bed by their family physician. Mr. W. went on to say he was sure Ray's stubbornness in regard to his intended marriage to Joan had brought on the attack. He asked Ray to call the engagement off so as not to further endanger Mrs. W's life.

It is a proverbial understatement to say that Ray was upset. He called Joan immediately and told her what his father had said. Joan asked Ray if he was willing to try something pretty "far out" to dissolve his parent's objection to their marriage. Ray agreed, and Joan followed the advice given to her by a friend some weeks previously, and telephoned me. We agreed on a time, and Joan and Ray paid me a visit.

"I'm willing to try anything," said Ray. "Nothing up to this point has changed my parents' minds even slightly. If this metacosmic projection can work, I'm all for it."

I went over the meta-cosmic projection technique they were to use to dissolve the objections Ray's parents had to their marriage They were to use the technique three times a day.

As they were leaving Ray said, "If this works, meta-cosmic projection can do anything."

Ten days later, I received a phone call from Ray.

"I can hardly believe what I've got to tell you," said Ray. "I got a call from my father last night and he and my mother have reconsidered their attitude toward my marriage to Joan. They've decided that if it makes me happy, they're all for it. In fact, since Joan's parents are both dead, my folks want to pay for a church wedding with all the trimmings. Can you believe that?"

I assured Ray that I had no trouble believing what he had told me.

"Oh, my mother is fine too," said Ray. "It wasn't really a heart attack. She just had herself upset. Anyway, she's fine now, and making plans for the wedding reception."

I shared his happiness and wished him well.

"By the way, Joan sends her thanks too," Ray said. "Meta-cosmic projection is terrific. Like I said, if it can get my parents' attitude to change, it can do anything."

The last time I heard from Ray and Joan W., they had just celebrated their first wedding anniversary and were getting alone fine with Ray's parents. In fact, the senior Mr. and Mrs. W. were anxiously awaiting the birth of their first grandchild who was due to arrive in five months.

Meta-Cosmic Projection Brings Stability to Marriage

As the divorce rate climbs, one can find more and more people who have been divorced and remarried three or even four times. George T. was such a person. George had been married and divorced four times and had recently entered his fifth marriage. His wife, Nancy, was twenty-five, twelve years younger than George. This was Nancy's first marriage, and she was determined that it should be successful. She had heard me speaking on a radio program and decided that she and her husband could use all the help they could get.

During our meeting, Nancy explained that she was well aware of George's marital history before she married him.

"I was in love with him and his past didn't matter," said Nancy. "Now, after a few months of marriage, I'm a little scared that I may end up as an ex-wife too. I don't want that to happen and neither does George."

George T. smiled at Nancy and then spoke to me. "Nancy is right. I want this marriage to work," George said. "She's told me a little about meta-cosmic projection. I don't completely understand it, but if it can help our marriage to work, I'd like to try it."

I explained the secrets of psychic binoculars and meta-cosmic projection. George and Nancy listened intently and said they would begin that very day by using their psychic binoculars to determine their needs and wants in marriage. Once they decided on those goals, they planned to use the secrets of meta-cosmic projection to attain them.

That was almost three years ago, and George and Nancy are looking forward to their fourth wedding anniversary and many many more after that. Both George and Nancy use meta-cosmic projection regularly and each states proudly that happiness is an everyday thing in their marriage.

Your Secret Technique for Deciding What You Need and Want in a Marriage

This technique is a variation of your basic psychic binoculars technique. You will need a piece of paper and a pen or pencil in order to perform this powerful exercise.

1. Write the following four words on your paper: "In marriage I want..."

2. Close your eyes, relax and mentally repeat the words "In marriage I want..."

Now complete that sentence with something you want in or from your marriage. Write your want on the paper directly after the words "In marriage I want..." For instance, if you want good communication in your marriage, the paper would read "In marriage I want good communication between me and my spouse."

3. Again write the words "In marriage I want..." on the paper. Once more close your eyes and mentally repeat the words "In marriage I want..." Write your second response on the paper.

4. For the third time write the words "In marriage I want..." on the paper. Close your eyes and mentally repeat the words "In marriage I want..." Write your third response on the paper.

5. Write the words "In marriage I need..." on the paper. Close your eyes and mentally repeat the words "In marriage I need..." Now complete the sentence and write your need on the paper. If you need your spouse to be demonstrative with affection, the paper will read, "In marriage I need my spouse to demonstrate affection often."

6. Write the words "In marriage I need..." once again and repeat step five. Write your second marital need on the paper.

7. For the third time write the words "In marriage I need..." on the paper and once again repeat step five.

Your paper should now contain six completed sentences, three sentences that state your marital wants, and three sentences that state your marital needs.

8. Read the three sentences in which you stated your marital wants. Now relax, close your eyes, and mentally repeat the marital wants you have listed. Listen to your own inner

voice and decide if the marital wants you have listed are truly things you want in or from your marriage. Are they goals for which you are willing to invest your time and energy?

9. Read the three sentences in which you stated your marital needs. Relax, close your eyes, and repeat mentally the marital needs you have listed. Again listen to your own inner voice and decide if your statements reflect real needs. Are the needs you listed necessary to your growth as a person?

This miraculous technique will allow you to know exactly what it is you want and need in a marital relationship. Once you have your goals clearly set, the secrets of meta-cosmic projection will allow you to attain each chosen goal.

Couple Set Their Goals with Psychic Binoculars

Unfortunately it is not uncommon in our society for couples who have been married for ten, fifteen, or twenty years to find themselves suddenly enmeshed in marital problems. Often as people grow their wants and needs change, and the individual who is unaware of this change may be truly considered at a disadvantage in a marriage. Neither we nor our world is static, and in order to maintain a happy marriage, or any relationship, we must be aware of those changes and identify our new wants and needs.

After sixteen years of marriage, Ken and Eileen J. found themselves in trouble. The things that had made their marriage a happy one for so many years no longer brought happiness. Neither could identify the problem or problems that were now threatening what had been a happy relationship.

"I'm not sure that this psychic binocular thing can help," said Ken, "but at this point, I'm willing to try anything."

We talked and I taught them the miraculous psychic binocular technique presented in this chapter.

"It sounds good," said Eileen, "but what do we do once we know what the problems are?"

I went on to explain the secrets of meta-cosmic projection. Ken and Eileen agreed to put both techniques to work in their lives.

In about two months, I received a call from Eileen.

"Those psychic binoculars are fantastic," she said. "In no time at all Ken and I were able to see what it was we both wanted and needed from our marriage. Once we had set our goals, the secret meta-cosmic technique you taught us worked like magic. Our marriage is better than ever! We plan to look through our psychic binoculars every so often and use meta-cosmic projection to keep our marriage happy and growing."

Meta-Cosmic Projection Can Give You the Marital Relationship You Want and Need

It is a wonderful fact that human beings are more alike than different. We all have dreams and goals, wants and needs, happy times and not-so-happy times. The miracle of meta-cosmic projection gives you the power to attain your goals and exchange the not-so-happy times of the past for happy times here and now.

The meta-cosmic technique for marital relationships, which follows, knows no limits to its power. It is yours to use today.

Your Meta-Cosmic Projection Technique for a Happy Marital Relationship

1. Read the list of marital wants and needs you have seen through your psychic binoculars.

2. Sit in a relaxed position, close your eyes, and recall your first want.

3. In your mind create a motion picture seeing and hearing yourself and your spouse in a situation in which your want is an actuality. See and hear yourself and your spouse saying *how happy you both are that your <u>want</u> is now a true reality in your life.*

4. *Recall your second marital <u>want</u> mentally.*

5. *In your mind again create a motion picture seeing and hearing yourself and your spouse in a situation in which your second <u>want</u> is an actuality. See and hear yourself and your spouse saying how happy you both are that your second <u>want</u> is now a true reality.*

6. *Repeat steps two and three for your third <u>want</u>.*

7. *Recall your first <u>need</u> mentally.*

8. *In your mind create a motion picture seeing and hearing yourself and your spouse in a situation in which your <u>need</u> is an actuality. See and hear yourself and your spouse saying how happy you both are that your <u>need</u> is now a true reality in your life.*

9. *Repeat steps seven and eight for your second <u>need</u>.*

10. *Repeat steps seven and eight for your third <u>need</u>.*

11. *Remain in a relaxed position with your eyes closed for approximately one minute.*

12. *Open your eyes and go about your daily life.*

Repeat this miraculous meta-cosmic projection three times a day. The quality of the time you spend in performing the technique is more important than the quantity of time you give to the technique. It is important that you give your full attention to each step in the technique each time you perform. Giving your full attention for ten or even five minutes is better than spending fifteen or twenty minutes performing the technique with inattention.

You now have the secret techniques of psychic binoculars and meta-cosmic projection that have the unlimited power to give you the exact marital relationship you seek. Who would be so foolish as not to use the unlimited power of those miraculous secrets? Put the secrets of meta-cosmic projection to work in your life today.

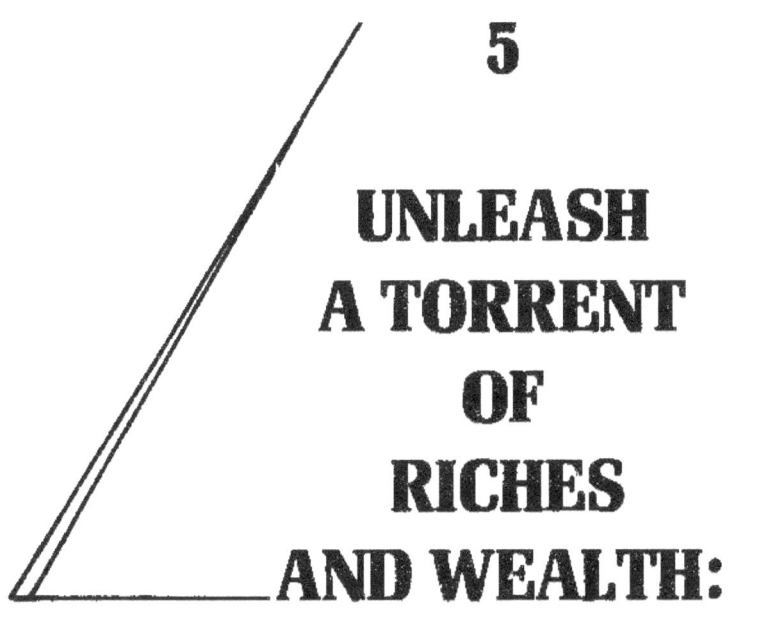

5
UNLEASH A TORRENT OF RICHES AND WEALTH:
Through Meta-Cosmic Projection

Most likely no one would deny that human beings have material needs and responsibilities as well as those that are non-material. Anyone who has worked for a living or managed a home on money provided by the breadwinner knows well that material needs and responsibilities are very real. The secrets of meta-cosmic projection are also very real. You can use the miracle of meta-cosmic projection to fill your material needs and wants.

The secrets of meta-cosmic projection can present you with opportunities to satisfy each and every one of your material needs and wants and can fatten your bank account in the process. There is absolutely no need for you to lack material rewards when the secrets of meta-cosmic projection presented in this chapter can bring those rewards into your life now.

Meta-Cosmic Projection Pays for a Trip to Europe

Jerry and Joan B. had married immediately after their college graduation. Both were hired as art teachers, and it took their combined salaries to keep their home going. Despite a tight squeeze to make ends meet, the young couple, over a two-year period, had managed to save almost twenty-five hundred dollars. They had earmarked the money for a summer vacation in Europe. Suddenly their plans for Europe fell apart. Following a visit to her doctor, Joan learned she was pregnant with their first child. Joan and her husband decided she would quit her job at the end of the term, which was three months away, and the money they had saved for Europe would go for the expenses that would follow the birth of their child. The small nest egg would also help to defray the loss of Joan's salary to the family.

It was not until after the birth of Jerry, Jr., that I met Mr. and Mrs. B. A friend had told them about meta-cosmic projection and they wanted to know if it could possibly pay their way to Europe.

"I guess it sounds frivolous to you," said Joan, "but we have both wanted this trip for so long that it really hurts not to be able to afford it. We both looked forward to seeing the art treasures and felt such a trip would aid our teaching."

I assured them that I didn't think their desire to visit Europe was at all frivolous. We then spent almost an hour talking about the meta-cosmic projection technique they were to use to finance their European tour. Summer break for Jerry was three months away, and they wanted to spend the summer in Europe.

Two months passed before I heard from the couple. Jerry called to tell me they were off to Europe for the summer.

"Everything is set," said Jerry. "We leave two weeks after the term ends. We'll spend the entire summer in Europe." After spilling over with excitement, Jerry explained how the money had come to them to pay for their trip.

"I've been hired as a representative for an art supply dealer. The company is paying all expenses for me, Joan, and the baby. My job is to travel to all the places in Europe I would have chosen to visit anyway. I'm to gather material and photos for a brochure the company will be putting out around January. In fact, if I do well with this assignment, we have a good chance of spending next summer in Europe on their payroll. It couldn't have turned out better. That meta-cosmic projection is an art treasure itself. It has created a beautiful summer for me and my family."

Meta-Cosmic Projection Works Just as Well at Home

Naturally everyone is not as anxious as Jerry and Joan B. to visit Europe. For many, many people, their material needs and wants revolve around their own homes. It doesn't matter whether your needs involve redecorating your apartment or building a dream house. The secrets of meta-cosmic projection can bring your material needs and wants into reality.

Psychic Binoculars Design a Dream House

Dan and Iris B. sought me out only after numerous arguments concerning the home they were planning to build. They had purchased the land on which to build their home, but could not agree on the style or construction for the house itself.

"It may sound like a small thing, but we've been having some pretty serious fights over it," said Dan. "I thought we both knew what we wanted, and I thought we were in agreement. Now it seems I was wrong on both counts. We've wasted almost a thousand dollars on two architectural blue prints we don't want to use. We can't afford to waste any more money, and the arguing is tearing us apart.

"We've heard about your psychic binocular technique and were hoping it could show us what we really wanted in a house — before we argue ourselves into a separation and don't need a dream house."

When Dan and Iris left they were determined to use their psychic binoculars to present their needs and wants accurately. They also planned to use meta-cosmic projection to get additional finance money for their house.

In two and a half months Dan and Iris stopped by to tell me that the foundation of their dream house had been poured and construction begun.

"We also got an okay at the bank for additional funds for construction," said Dan. "We are now staunch advocates of psychic binoculars and meta-cosmic projection."

Meta-Cosmic Projection Can Put You in the Driver's Seat

When Ron O. visited me for the first time he was somewhat apologetic concerning the reason for his visit.

"I've heard quite a bit about meta-cosmic projection bringing people material things they needed, but I want to use it for something I don't really need. I want a new car, but I can't truthfully say I need one," said Ron. "My present car is only three years old, and it's in fine condition. I have no real complaints with it, but I really want a new car. Is it okay to use meta-cosmic projection for a want instead of a need?"

I assured Ron that there was nothing wrong with using meta-cosmic projection to fill a material want and we discussed the technique he was to use. In the time we talked I made it very clear that the chances were very great against him finding a gift-wrapped new car with his name on it just sitting in front of his door one morning. *The way meta-cosmic projection works is to provide the opportunities* that will allow you to achieve your material needs and wants. Ron said he understood and was determined to follow the meta-cosmic projection technique I had outlined.

Two weeks later Ron phoned. "How would you like to go for a ride in my new car?" he asked. "I just got it last night. It seems a bank had ordered it for an executive who was transferred before he could take delivery. A friend of mine at the bank told me about it. The car was exactly what I wanted and they were willing to take a fantastic loss on it and finance it besides. I sold my car for a good price and bought the new one yesterday afternoon. I was behind the wheel by 5:30 p.m. It's a real beauty. You'd think it was ordered just for me — the color, accessories — everything is exactly what I wanted."

Ron paused only long enough to catch his breath. "Meta-cosmic projection is absolutely terrific. It works miracles like magic."

I declined the ride but congratulated Ron on his new car. Meta-cosmic projection had put him in the driver's seat.

Meta-Cosmic Projection Can Lead You to a Sale

Jan W. had not dropped in to ask about sales, but in the course of our conversation the subject came up.

"I don't doubt that meta-cosmic projection works, but can it get me more for my money?" asked Jan. "I need to buy the kids new school clothes, and I have so much budgeted for that purpose. If I can get the same or better quality clothes that I usually buy on sale, I can get more for my money."

After we talked, Jan decided to shop on sale with the help of meta-cosmic projection. One week later I received a call from her.

"Well, it worked as usual," she said. "I found a terrific sale and doubled my purchasing power. The kids are tickled to have extra clothes they didn't expect, and naturally I'm happy to have gotten more for my money without sacrificing quality."

Psychic Binoculars Can Lead to a Full Refrigerator

Don and Betty H. were also looking for a bargain. With increasing food prices, Don and Betty were interested in stretching their food dollar without compromising quality.

"We have five children," said Don. "Feeding the family is taking more and more of my paycheck. I don't want to bring inferior food home, but if this psychic binocular thing can show us how to get more for our money, I'm all for it. That is as long as we stay with the same quality or do better quality-wise."

I taught them both how to use their psychic binoculars. In three weeks I heard from Betty.

"This psychic binocular thing is great," she said. "We have been finding one sale after another. I already have three of my neighbors who want to know my secret of finding sales. I'm teaching them to use their psychic binoculars while they shop with me. We're all eating better, enjoying it more, and it's costing us less. It sure beats the high cost of food."

The same secrets that allowed Don and Betty H. to fill their refrigerator at sale prices are available to you in this chapter.

Meta-Cosmic Projection Fills Entertainment Need

Enjoyment can be a real need and a real want. Meta-cosmic projection can fill these needs and wants completely. One need not hesitate to use this miraculous power to increase his enjoyment of life. Life is a great gift — so great, in fact, that the only way to say "thank you" for that gift is to live life fully. Living life fully includes enjoying it.

Meta-Cosmic Projection Brings Color TV

Tom K. had his doubts as to whether enjoyment of life was a legitimate need or want. For most of his life, Tom had believed that enjoying anything was just a "lucky extra." Now he wasn't so sure — maybe enjoying life was something one could aim at and work to achieve.

"My family has wanted a color TV for quite a while," said Mr. K. "About a week ago, I took a chance on winning a color TV and, when my friend told me about meta-cosmic projection, I decided to see if I could win it. Will you teach me to use meta-cosmic projection so I can win the TV for my family? I know we don't really need it, but it's something they have wanted for a long time."

I agreed to teach Mr. K. the use of meta-cosmic projection and, since the drawing was in one week, he was more than anxious to learn. He left agreeing to use the techniques I had taught him no more than three times a day.

Ten days passed before I received a call from Mr. K.

"Our color TV was delivered this morning," he said. "I wasn't even surprised when they called to tell me I had won. I just knew I would. That meta-cosmic projection is wonderful. I intend to use it regularly from now on in my life."

The Secrets Are Yours Today

The very secrets of meta-cosmic projection and psychic binoculars that have helped thousands of other people to reach their goals are yours to use this very day. The meta-cosmic projection technique provided for you in this chapter can fill all your material needs and wants.

Before you begin this miraculous exercise for the fulfillment of your material needs, you should use your psychic binoculars, as you have already learned in earlier chapters, to determine exactly what your needs and wants are at this point in your life. Once you have identified those needs and wants, you can use the miraculous exercise provided in this chapter that will bring fulfillment to your needs and wants.

Make your psychic binoculars and the meta-cosmic projection technique which follows, the first stop on your way to reaching your material goals. It will allow you to unlock powers within yourself that may have laid dormant all your life.

Your Meta-Cosmic Projection Technique for Fulfillment of Material Needs and/or Wants

1. Use your psychic binoculars to determine exactly what constitute your material needs and wants.

2. Sit in a relaxed position, close your eyes, and give your attention to your breathing. Make no attempt to control your breathing, merely keep it in your awareness for one minute.

3. In your own mind create a motion picture in which you see yourself in possession of the fulfillment of your material need or want. Hear yourself saying, "This is wonderful, I have received exactly what I wanted."

4. Now extend your motion picture and see and hear members of your family and/or friends congratulating you on your new material successes.

5. See and hear yourself accepting these congratulations graciously.

6. See and hear yourself enjoying your newly acquired material possession. For example, if you are using this technique to acquire a new car, see yourself driving that new car, and hear friends complimenting you on its wonderful features.

7. Relax and allow your mind to remain open to silence. Again, for sixty seconds, put your attention on your breathing. Now go about the regular activities of your day.

Repeat this technique three times a day.

The secrets of meta-cosmic projection have the power to fill each one of your material needs. Begin today to use your secret meta-cosmic projection technique to obtain your material needs and wants.

6

EMOTIONAL CONTROL THROUGH META-COSMIC PROJECTION:

Learn to be super-cool at all times

If you have ever suffered emotional upsets, or watched, feeling helpless, as a friend or relative suffered emotional anguish, the secrets of meta-cosmic projection contained in this chapter hold an important key for you.

There are many books, movies, and TV shows that portray as their main theme the events in the life of a depressed individual. Depression is also discussed on radio and TV talk shows, since it is a topic that touches the lives of countless human beings. Psychologists know that anger and hostility, turned inward, often lead to depression so severe as to paralyze the life of an individual. Some physicians prescribe medications known commonly as "mood elevators" to combat the agonies of depression. Ironically, some individuals are further depressed at the thought of being dependent on a tablet or capsule in order to feel good. It isn't too difficult to understand the depression sometimes generated by a reliance on artificial means to ease the pains this depression brings. Too frequently depression generates depression and an individual finds himself caught on an emotional treadmill. Pills that elevate moods for a brief period of time do nothing to combat the underlying causes of depression.

The secrets of meta-cosmic projection have the power to cure depression at its source. Depression crumbles before these miraculous secrets as easily as papier-mache under the force of a steam roller. Meta-cosmic projection provides you with a natural means of overcoming depression without running the risks of the side effects inherent in many medications.

Woman Overcomes Depression

When I think about my first meeting with Sarah T. I am astounded by the fact that she mobilized herself enough to seek help. The tone of her voice, the stoop of her shoulders, and an unmistakable dullness in her eyes declared her depression. She spoke slowly and in a powder-dry voice.

"I'm not sure you can help me, but I've tried everything else," said Sarah. "I've been to four different doctors and have taken about ten different kinds of medicine that were supposed to help my depression. So far, nothing has helped for more than a week at a time. I'm tired of taking pills that don't work for me — I'm tired of paying for them, too."

Sarah went on to say that she had suffered moderate to severe depression for the past six years. During that time she had only brief periods of relief and those periods became more brief as her body developed a tolerance for the particular mood elevator she was taking. A new medication was then prescribed and the cycle of relief began again, always to end as its predecessor — replaced by a new mood elevator.

"Living this way is depressing by itself," said Sarah. "My teenage son laughs when I warn him against drugs. He considers me a kind of emotional addict. I can't really blame him. My day is crowded with pills and my case history would run pretty parallel to the developmental history of mood elevators. If it's out, I've tried it. If it's coming out, it will probably be prescribed for me next week."

Sarah paused only briefly. "I'm tired of taking pills and not really getting anyplace. I've heard a little about meta-cosmic projection from a friend and I want to know if it can help me."

I explained to Sarah that if she were willing to perform the meta-cosmic projection technique and carry it out faithfully as directed, her depression could be cured completely. She agreed to do her part and left an hour later saying she would keep me informed of her progress. Suddenly she turned and said, "...or my lack of progress." That statement led to a 20 minute conversation concerning negative thinking, and Sarah, left on what was, for her, a positive note.

After two weeks passed with no word from Sarah, I wondered if she had decided not to try meta-cosmic projection. Three more weeks were to pass before Sarah telephoned. At first I didn't recognize the enthusiastic voice that bubbled from the phone.

"Congratulate me," she said. "My depression is cured."

I said I was happy for her and she continued to speak.

"It took about two and a half weeks for me to accept the fact that I wan't depressed any more. That was after two days of arguing with myself as to whether meta-cosmic projection could really work. Once I accepted that it could work, things moved pretty fast. If I hadn't continued to look for my depression, I would have realized even sooner that it was gone."

Sarah paused and laughed. "Would you believe I just

couldn't stand feeling good at first. I actually argued myself back into depression three times before I wised up."

I told Sarah that unfortunately many people actively look for their problems at first while using meta-cosmic projection. People waste a lot of their own time looking for problems that have already gone.

"Well, once I got over that, things really started looking up," she said. "I've been on a two week vacation, my first in six years, and I had a ball. Everything is just great. I feel so good I'm not even going to spend time worrying about the time I wasted over the last six years, although I do wish that I had known about meta-cosmic projection back then. Anyway everything is super now."

Sarah T's. depression had crumbled under the force of meta-cosmic projection. That same miraculous force is available to you in the secrets of meta-cosmic projection contained in this chapter.

Your Psychic Binoculars Can Show You the Person You Want to Be

Few, if any, psychologists would argue the fact that the way a person sees himself is of extreme importance. Unless an individual sees himself as successful, it is unlikely that anyone else will see him as a success. The way a person sees himself affects the way he interacts with others. Many unconscious and unspoken messages, based on a person's self-image, are conveyed by individuals as to how they expect to be treated by their fellow human beings. That self-image is of the utmost importance to every person on this planet. Through the use of the miraculous power of your psychic binoculars, you can see yourself as the successful person you want to be, and once you have that image clearly in view, meta-cosmic projection can do the rest.

Man Gains New Self-Respect Through the Use of His Psychic Binoculars

Ted R. had many of the world's marks of success in his life. One thing he didn't have was a respect for himself and an inner feeling that he was in any sense a successful human being.

"I really don't know why I'm talking to you!" said Ted at our first meeting. "In a way I'm probably wasting your time. I just don't seem to be able to do anything right. I have a good job, but I'm sure if my bosses really knew me, I'd be fired. I'm sure it's just luck that I've been able to get things accomplished. I know I don't feel like I have anything to offer at work or in my personal life. In fact, I feel that people who did trust my judgment before are beginning to doubt it now."

I suggested to Ted that perhaps the fact that he didn't trust himself was reaching others through unconscious messages sent by him.

"I guess it's possible," Ted agreed. "How do I change it? I've heard of this meta-cosmic projection stuff. Will it work for me?"

I assured Ted that meta-cosmic projection would work for him, but suggested he use his psychic binoculars first to see himself as he would have himself be. We talked about the use of psychic binoculars and meta-cosmic projection and Ted promised himself to use the techniques faithfully.

Three weeks later I received a phone call from Ted.

"You are talking to a new man," said Ted. "For the first time in years I have confidence in myself and in my ideas. I guess it shows, because people have been responding to me a lot differently. I can tell that they respect and trust me now. This thing about developing a good self-image is terrific! It goes without saying that the power of psychic binoculars and meta-cosmic projection is absolutely fantastic. Thanks to those secret techniques, I feel like a million dollars."

The same techniques that worked for Ted R. can work just as effectively for you. Those secrets of meta-cosmic projection and psychic binoculars are waiting for you in this chapter. You have only to follow the techniques faithfully in order to become the person you want to be.

Woman Changed Her Life with the Secrets of Meta-Cosmic Projection

Virginia G. was visibly upset when she first visited me. Virginia had begun to go through the menopause six months earlier and had suffered from raw nerves and depression. She was unable to take estrogen due to an adverse reaction to the drug.

"It's not just that *I'm* miserable," said Virginia. "I'm making my family miserable, too. My nerves stay so on edge that I snap at every remark. They're not even safe if they remain silent, since I snap at them for not wanting to talk to me."

She forced a smile and spoke quietly. "I've tried everything. Everything but meta-cosmic projection that is. I want you to teach me how to use meta-cosmic projection so I can be happy and allow my family to be happy."

One month later Virginia was on the telephone. "Meta-cosmic projection is wonderful," she said. "I haven't been at all jumpy. I feel great and so does my family. There are millions of households in this country that could benefit from learning just this one technique. You can bet I'll tell everyone I know about it."

Virginia G. is one of many women and families who have problems stemming from the menopause. She returned to a happy life through the secrets of meta-cosmic projection, as have countless other women and their families. The same secrets are yours today in this very chapter.

Meta-Cosmic Prayer Is Not Bound by Any Creed

One definition of prayer might be to want good things for yourself and/or for others. To seek the good for anyone is a prayer and to back your seeking of that good with an act of your ever-powerful will is meta-cosmic prayer.

Meta-cosmic prayer is much more than words and much more than wanting good for yourself or another. It is the unique combination of words combined with an act of the will, forcefully willing that good be poured upon yourself and upon those for whom you pray.

Meta-cosmic prayer involves a strong act of faith. It involves a firm belief in and recognition of the limitless power of the intellect and will. With this knowledge and willful act of the intellect, the meta-cosmic prayer is born. When you pray a meta-cosmic prayer, you can always be sure it will be answered.

Family United Through the Prayer of Meta-Cosmic Projection

Brian B.'s family had once been close-knit and happy. When Brian visited me, however, it was because his family had been torn by depression, self-doubt and unreasonable hostility of family member toward family member.

"It's hard to believe we're the same family," said Brian B. "We used to get along fine, now we barely speak to each other. It all started when my wife, Ann, began the menopause. She got very edgy and because of the controversy about estrogen, she didn't want to take it at first, and our two sons were pretty patient with Ann. Our patience didn't seem to help, though. She got crankier and crankier. We just couldn't win. It's that way now, we're damned if we do and damned if we don't."

Mr. B. paused and seemed to gather his thoughts. "Eventually the boys began yelling back at their mother or avoiding her as much as possible," he said. "I'm afraid I took the same tack. In fact, that's where we are now. We're no longer a family. Everybody is jumpy and defensive. I talked to the boys but it's gotten to the point where we're cranky with each other too. It's as though we're all too depressed and too battle-shy to try any more."

Brian paused again and took a deep breath. "I want my family the way it used to be," he said. "I thought you might be able to teach me meta-cosmic projection. I've heard of it, but, to tell you the truth, I lean more to prayer."

I explained to Mr. B. that he could use a miracle prayer of meta-cosmic projection. He agreed a little reluctantly to give it a try.

Five weeks later, Mr. B. paid me another visit.

"That prayer of meta-cosmic projection worked great. My family is the way we used to be, only better," Brian said. "Ann isn't edgy any more, and the boys and I have gotten over being jumpy and battle-shy. It's as if all the depression and self-doubt that had torn us apart have just melted away. I have always known that prayer is powerful, but this prayer of meta-cosmic projection is almost unbelievable. It really works!"

Meta-Cosmic Projection Can Help Your Unbelief

In the many years I have worked with people I have found that the lack of faith has acted as a huge stumbling block for people on their path to their goal. Faith is a simple act of trust, and yet that act of trust is often difficult for many people. We are told in the sacred books of many religions that "...faith can move mountains" and that "...your faith has made you whole." What a powerful, powerful act is this simple act of belief!

Faith can be gained in many ways and one of those ways is simply to ask for it. Perhaps one of the most efficient prayers for faith can be found in the New Testament lines "Lord, I do believe. Help thou my unbelief."

The secrets of meta-cosmic projection can help your unbelief just as they have helped the unbelief of so many others.

Man Gains Deep Faith Through Meta-Cosmic Projection

Paul M. was a man who really wanted to believe in himself, in his family, in his ideas and in something or someone greater than man.

"My problem," Paul explained, "is that I don't believe in anything or anybody. At least I don't believe that people won't knife you in the back if it will net them a nickel."

Paul went on to explain that he was not happy with his attitude toward life and had tried many times, unsuccessfully, to change it.

"Nothing works," he said. "People have never proved me wrong. Where a dollar or a little status is involved, they'll cut your throat as soon as say 'hello.'" He paused briefly. "I hope you're not going to tell me to turn the other cheek. I've tried that too. All I got was laughed at for being so stupid."

Finally Paul came to the reason for his visit. "I want you to teach me meta-cosmic projection so I can start trusting people. I just can't go on like this, with no faith in myself or anyone else. In fact, if you know any good prayers you'd better teach me those too. I'm not sure I trust you or your meta-cosmic projection."

I taught Paul M. a meta-cosmic prayer and a meta-cosmic projection technique for the acquisition of deep faith. Without expressing much belief in the prayer or the technique, he agreed to use both.

Two months passed without one word from Paul. One morning the phone rang and Paul filled me in on his past two months.

"I fought with myself for at least two weeks before I really began following your instructions," he said. "I began with the prayer at first, then gradually I began to have faith that the meta-cosmic projection would work for me. Well, believe me, it did work. I began taking the chance of trusting people and I'll be darned, if they didn't live up to my trust in them!

"I also began trusting my own ideas. You know something, my ideas also worked. My whole life just seemed to fall into place. It's just great trusting myself and others. I've also begun to attend church regularly. My entire life has changed due to my faith. Faith really is a simple act of trust, but I'm sure glad I had a meta-cosmic prayer and meta-cosmic projection to help me make that simple act of trust a real force in my life."

Your Meta-Cosmic Prayer for Faith

Pray this meta-cosmic prayer three times a day. It is impossible for it to go unanswered.

MAY MY MIND BE OPEN TO THE BEAUTY THAT SURROUNDS ME EACH DAY. MY MIND IS OPEN TO THE BEAUTY THAT SURROUNDS ME EACH DAY.

MY EYES BEHOLD THE KINDNESSES EACH DAY IN MY OWN LIFE AND IN THE LIVES OF OTHERS.

MY EARS HEAR THE LOVE WHICH FILLS EVERY DAY WITH WARMTH AND CARING.

I AM AWARE OF THE GOODNESS OF THE EARTH ON WHICH I WALK, AND OF THE SKY THAT SHELTERS ME.

I AM AWARE OF THE GOODNESS IN MY OWN HEART AND IN THE HEARTS OF MY FELLOWS.

Your Meta-Cosmic Projection
Technique for Renewed and Deep Faith

Repeat this technique three times a day. It has brought renewed and deep faith to countless people and it will do the same for you.

1. *Sit or lie in a quiet place.*

2. *Close your eyes and give your full attention to your breathing. Do not attempt to control your breath, but simply watch the intake and outflow of your breathing.*

3. *Create a mental picture of yourself. See and hear yourself saying to a friend or family member, "I have a whole new outlook on life. I just know that things always turn out right. I have a deep faith in myself and in life."*

4. *See and hear your friend or family member saying, "I can really see the change in you. Your new faith in yourself and others has really made you happy."*

5. *Again give your attention to your breathing for approximately thirty seconds.*

6. *Open your eyes and go about your daily life.*

Your Light Can Brighten the World

The secrets of meta-cosmic projection can brighten the entire world. Countless numbers of people have used these miraculous techniques to bring emotional peace to themselves and their loved ones. Just think! The more who use the secrets of meta-cosmic projection for their own life, the brighter the world is for everyone.

Start today! Let the secrets of meta-cosmic projection bring emotional peace to you and your loved ones, then watch it flow forth to brighten your entire world.

7

HEALING THROUGH META-COSMIC PROJECTION:

Magic curative powers for your body.

You can be as healthy as you want to be. The secrets of meta-cosmic projection can heal physical illness as well as emotional upsets. There is absolutely no need for you to spend another day in physical suffering, for the secrets of meta-cosmic projection presented to you in this chapter can heal that suffering now.

Even those who suffered from seemingly helpless illnesses have regained their health through the miraculous secrets of meta-cosmic projection. The power of meta-cosmic projection knows no limits. The only force that can block the awesome power of meta-cosmic projection is your own refusal to use these miraculous secrets. Meta-cosmic projection knows nothing that can stop its miraculous force. Begin today to put that force to work in your own life.

Woman Cured Through the Secrets of Meta-Cosmic Projection

Emily V. had suffered from asthma for fifteen years. Her physician had prescribed various medications in an attempt to control the terrible attacks that robbed her of breath. In spite of these medicines, Emily V. suffered numerous asthmatic attacks that racked her body and disorganized her daily life.

As the mother of two young children, Emily found her illness a hinderance to happy family life.

"I can't begin to count the number of times family plans had to be changed due to one of my asthma attacks," Emily said. Her voice was sad and heavy as she spoke of cancelled outings, cancelled parties and cancelled trips, each denied her family and herself because of a sudden asthmatic seizure.

"I'm just plain tired of this thing," she said. "I want to live a normal life and I don't want my family to suffer because of me. Not that they've ever complained — they haven't — but I want them to be able to enjoy family togetherness without worrying about a sudden cancellation due to my asthma attacks.

"Two of my girlfriends have told me about meta-cosmic projection and suggested that I talk to you. To be quite honest, I'm not sure it will help — nothing else has — but I'd like you to teach me meta-cosmic projection to heal my asthma attacks."

We talked for an hour or so, and Emily left determined to use meta-cosmic projection to rid herself of the attacks that had disorganized her personal and family life.

It was seven weeks before I heard from Emily again. She and her family had taken a three-week vacation and enjoyed every minute of it.

"This was the first vacation I can remember where my asthma attacks didn't interfere," said Emily. "I haven't had an attack in five weeks. My doctor is real happy for me. He's cut my medication in half and says that if I continue to be free of attacks, he'll cut it further. He'll be surprised when he finds he can stop it altogether. That will be a red-letter day in my life, and I know it isn't far off. Meta-cosmic projection is the most wonderful force to come into my life yet!"

Emily V. had learned what countless others had learned before her, that meta-cosmic projection can heal the body and restore health where it seems hopelessly lost.

Your Psychic Binoculars Can Allow You to Bring Health to Others

The secrets of meta-cosmic projection hold a force that is not bound to personal use. You can use the miraculous power of meta-cosmic projection to restore health to your loved ones and friends. No longer need you wish that you had the power to ease the suffering of a loved one and restore that individual to health. That power is yours today! The miraculous secrets of meta-cosmic projection put this unlimited power at your command this very moment.

Man Uses Psychic Binoculars and Meta-Cosmic Projection to Cure His Wife of Ulcers

When John B. first visited me he was a frustrated, angry man. His wife, Helen, had suffered from stomach ulcers for three years. She had been hospitalized twice for ulcers before they moved to Georgia, and her life was greatly restricted due to her condition. As is true of so many illnesses, Helen found that ulcers led to other complications in her life. It had been necessary to restrict her diet drastically and this restriction had affected John also.

"I just don't feel right eating things at home that I know Helen can't eat," John said. "In my business we have to attend quite a few dinners and Helen is sometimes embarrassed by having to pass on particular foods that just aren't good for her ulcers."

John hesitated a moment and I could feel the frustration he was experiencing at wanting to help his wife and yet not knowing how to go about it.

"She won't ask you for help herself," he said. "She is awfully shy and pretty depressed at not finding the help she needs before now. She asked me to find out about meta-cosmic projection for her. One of her friends told her a little about the technique, but at the time, Helen wasn't ready to listen. I'm not sure she's ready now, but I figured if meta-cosmic projection is as strong as it will have to be to get rid of Helen's ulcers, then I can use it for her. It is that strong, isn't it?"

I assured John that meta-cosmic projection knew no limits on its power and that he could very well use it in his wife's behalf. We talked about psychic binoculars, and I taught John to use his own psychic binoculars to see what he and his wife really wanted changed in their life. Once he had viewed their situation through his psychic binoculars, he made a quick phone call to his wife to tell her what he saw as things to be healed in their lives. Helen agreed after expressing amazement that he had put her feelings so well into words.

"Those psychic binoculars are fantastic," said John. "I was never so sure before about the changes my wife and I both want in our lives."

We went on to discuss the secrets of meta-cosmic projection and John left vowing to use the technique three times a day to bring healing to his wife's ulcers.

One month later I received a call from Helen B. Even as she introduced herself the excitement in her voice was evident.

"I got the word from my doctor yesterday," Helen said. "My ulcers are completely healed. My doctor is dumbfounded, but very happy for me. He's taken me off my special diet and ulcer medicine. For the first time in three years, I can eat what I want and not worry about an ulcer attack.

"John is standing right here with me, but I wanted to thank you myself for teaching him to use meta-cosmic projection. Not only have my ulcers been healed, but our whole life has become happier."

Perhaps the healing of ulcers through meta-cosmic projection illustrates, as well as or better than any other cure, the awesome power that is man's to cure illnesses which seem incapable of being healed or are strongly resistant to a cure. This wonderful power is at your fingertips through the secrets of meta-cosmic projection.

Man Cured of Paralysis Through Meta-Cosmic Projection

Jim S. had suffered a stroke that left the left side of his body almost completely paralyzed. He was able to drag his left foot with great effort and his left arm and hand were practically useless.

Jim was in a wheelchair when he visited me, and he made it very clear that he wanted to be free of that chair for good.

"The way I see it," Jim said, "life is too precious to be stuck in a wheelchair. I may be 68 years old, but my mind is as sharp as a tack. I still have a lot of living to do and I don't want to be held back by paralysis. Teach me how to use meta-cosmic projection so I can get out of this chair for good and get back to the pleasure of living every day fully."

I couldn't help being moved by Jim's attitude toward life. At 68 he was younger and more alive than many people I had met who were chronologically only in their 20's or 30's. Jim S. appreciated life, and so had always found it an exciting adventure.

He listened with eager ears and mind as I explained the use of meta-cosmic projection to him. There wasn't a doubt in Jim's mind that meta-cosmic projection would heal his paralysis and give him the full use of his limbs once again. He left promising me the first dance once he was out of his wheelchair for good.

Three weeks later, Jim visited me again, this time without the wheelchair and completely under his own power. He was carrying a portable radio, and I should have guessed immediately what it was for. After we talked for a half hour or so about his healing, Jim smiled and switched on an FM station. His smile spread as he bowed slightly and spoke in a serious but happy voice.

"I believe this waltz is mine," he said. Without my speaking a word, we waltzed around the front of the classroom where we had been talking. A few students hurrying to classes heard the music as they passed the open door. They stopped for a moment to watch a handsome gentleman of 68 guide his somewhat less adept partner with a grace that seemed to flow from him as easily as the notes of the Strauss waltz.

Man Uses Meta-Cosmic Projection to Regain the Use of His Right Arm

"My right arm is practically useless," said Victor M. during his first visit with me. "The doctors say I have a damaged nerve, and that stops my muscles from working as they should." He went on to explain that he had been suffering from this condition for almost two years.

"I'm tired of the darn thing," he said emphatically. "Physical therapy helped a little but not nearly enough. I want the full use of my arm again. How about teaching me that healing technique I've heard about. Meta something or other..."

"Meta-cosmic projection," I said.

"Yeah, that's it. I've heard about it from some friends and

I want you to teach me to use it. How about it, will you help me to help myself?"

I agreed and we talked about meta-cosmic projection for some time.

Six weeks later Victor phoned me. "I don't think you'll be surprised to hear that my arm is just fine. That meta-cosmic projection is powerful stuff."

I might not have chosen those exact words, but I surely couldn't argue with Victor. Meta-cosmic projection is a miraculously powerful force.

Arthritis Is No Match for the Secrets of Meta-Cosmic Projection

Phyllis H. wanted to learn meta-cosmic projection to cure her arthritic pain. She told me that she had suffered from moderate to severe arthritic pain in her knees and hands for eight years.

"If there's any medicine for arthritis that I haven't tried, it must have been put on the market within the last ten minutes, Phyllis said. "I'm just so tired of the pain and the limits it puts on my activities that I could scream. I love to knit and at times my arthritis pain is so bad that I can't even handle the knitting needles."

After my talking about the secrets of meta-cosmic projection, Phyllis was anxious to put them to work in her life.

A month passed before I heard from Phyllis again. Her voice was exuberant.

"I have just finished knitting an afghan that I have been trying to finish for more than a year," Phyllis said. "My arthritis hasn't bothered me in three weeks. In fact, all the swelling is gone. It's just wonderful to be free to do what I want again after eight years of almost constant pain. I just wish I had known about meta-cosmic projection years ago."

Phyllis had discovered what so many others have also discovered, that arthritis is no match for meta-cosmic projection. You can use the same meta-cosmic projection technique to free yourself, a friend, or a loved one from arthritic pain this very day.

The Miraculous Meta-Cosmic Projection Technique That Allows You to Claim Your Perfect Health

This miraculous technique of meta-cosmic projection should be used three times a day. The amount of time you spend practicing the technique is not as important as the quality of time you spend. If your mind begins to wander during any of the steps, discontinue the exercise and carry it out at another time. It is very important that your full awareness be placed on the technique while you carry it out.

1. Select a place where you are not likely to be disturbed. If possible, take the receiver of the telephone off its cradle while you are performing the exercise. This will rule out unexpected interruptions through phone calls.

2. Lie down or sit in a chair with a back high enough to support your head.

3. For approximately thirty seconds, put all your awareness on your own breathing. Close your eyes and mentally watch the intake and outflow of your own breathing.

4. Take a deep breath, and as you exhale, relax your stomach muscles completely. Repeat this step three times. Each time you inhale, imagine that you see the oxygen you have breathed in traveling to all the cells in your body.

5. In your mind's eye, see or imagine your physical illness. For example, if your illness is stomach ulcers, see or imagine your own stomach with the ulcers present. (You might consult a home medical book if you do not know what a stomach or a stomach ulcer looks like. You might also ask your medical doctor to describe your condition for you in order that you may see the condition clearly in your mind.)

6. With the mental picture of your illness held in your mind's eye, see or imagine a very bright white light flooding the afflicted area. Now see the disease disappearing and the organs and cells returning to a healthy condition. *(You may also wish to consult a home medical book or your physician in order to get a clear picture for yourself of what your body cells and organs should look like when they are healthy.)* For example, if you have formed the picture of one ulcerated place in your stomach, begin to see the ulcer shrink in size until it disappears completely and only healthy tissue remains.

7. For approximately thirty seconds, hold this image of perfect health in your consciousness. See yourself, or imagine yourself, completely free of illness. See healthy cells and organs in your body.

8. Mentally say the following words: "I accept my own perfect health. I command my body to destroy all diseased or injured cells within me and to replace them immediately with healthy cells free of all disease or injury." *(Your own words may be substituted, but the meaning must remain the same.)*

9. See or imagine yourself talking with your physician. See and hear your doctor saying the following words: "Your illness is completely cured. You are now in perfect health." *(Again, you may substitute your own words, but be sure to maintain the same meaning.)*

10. See or imagine yourself answering your doctor with the following words: "Thank you, doctor. I am very happy to be free of illness and in perfect health." *(If you substitute your own words, be sure to keep the same meaning.)*

11. Again place all your awareness on your own breathing for approximately thirty seconds.

12. Open your eyes and go about your daily life.

It is most important that you check with your physician according to the directions your doctor gives you. When your healing takes place, visit your physician in order that your healing may be verified and documented.

The secrets of meta-cosmic projection for healing the body are now your very own. You need only follow the simple steps in the miraculous technique given in this chapter in order to be able to claim your perfect health. Don't waste another day in needless pain. Begin now to use the secrets of meta-cosmic projection in order that you too may claim the blessing of perfect health.

8

THE POWER OF META-COSMIC PROJECTION:

Tyrants and enemies cannot harm you or your loved ones.

Perhaps an ideal situation will exist one day when no one has enemies. In the world in which you and I live today, however, it is safe to bet that few people, if any, have no enemies. When an individual holds strong convictions, and is willing to stand by those convictions, it is unlikely that everyone will respond favorably to him or her. It is necessary, therefore, to protect yourself from enemies, and the secrets of meta-cosmic projection can give you power over your enemies.

The secrets of meta-cosmic projection can make you stronger than any foe. Even if your enemies are unknown to you, the power of your psychic binoculars and the secrets of meta-cosmic projection can protect you from their negative thoughts and actions.

Man Uses His Psychic Binoculars to Overcome His Secret Enemies

Joseph W. was in perfect physical health, but greatly confused when he visited me for the first time. Unexpected events had been plaguing his life for three months.

"I just don't understand it," said Joseph. "For the past three months, deals that I thought were sure things have fallen through at the last minute. At first I thought I was slipping, and I probably would have stayed with that thought if just one or two deals had fallen through. I can't buy that idea any longer. Too many deals have gone sour."

Joseph's frustration and confusion were very apparent.

"I've been the top salesman of my company for two years," Joseph said. "In fact, just four months ago, I was told that I'm being considered for a promotion to an area sales manager's job that will be open in three more months. The way things have been going, I'll be lucky to keep my present job."

Joseph hesitated as if he didn't really want to speak his next thought.

"I really hate to say this," he said, "but a buddy of mine had told me that someone in the company is trying to make me look bad. My buddy doesn't know who it is, but he has it on good authority that someone has deliberately been lousing up my deals. I just can't imagine who would do that to me. No one else is up for the area manager's job, so it can't be anyone trying to get the job away from me. I just can't imagine who my enemy is."

We talked for an hour or so about the power of psychic binoculars and the secrets of meta-cosmic projection. Joseph agreed to use his psychic binoculars to determine exactly how he wanted the situation resolved. Once Joseph had decided on the resolution he wanted, he was to use the secrets of meta-cosmic projection to protect himself from his enemies.

Two weeks later I received a phone call from Joseph.

"I'm afraid you're not going to believe this," Joseph said. "It sounds crazy, but the two guys who were trying to do me in changed their minds. They both came to me the day before yesterday and, sort of, apologized for messing up my deals. They didn't come right out and admit what they had been doing, but it was clear what they were talking about. Both of them said they heard I'd been having some bad luck with my sales deals and would do whatever they could to help me.

"It didn't take them very long. Yesterday I had three deals, that had been cancelled, reinstated. This morning I had two companies call to place orders they had cancelled two weeks ago."

Joseph went on to explain that the two men who had offered their help were both area managers who weren't too sure they wanted Joseph for a colleague. They had formed a dislike for him based on their misunderstanding of his sales methods and goals. They both deliberately sabotaged Joseph's sales deals and planned to sabotage his chances for promotion. Then suddenly their attitude changed, and not only did they stop sabotaging him, but were determined to be of help.

"My enemies were no match for meta-cosmic projection," said Joseph. "Not only are they no longer out to hurt me, but thanks to meta-cosmic projection, they actually want to help me."

Several months later, I received another call from Joseph. He had been promoted to area manager and wanted me to know that he was using meta-cosmic projection regularly and his life was going great.

The very same secrets of meta-cosmic projection that protected Joseph W. from his enemies are available to you this very moment. The invincible power that will protect you from your enemies is now at your fingertips and awaits you in this very chapter.

Meta-Cosmic Projection Can Protect Your Entire Family

The invincible power of meta-cosmic projection can protect not only you, but can be used by you to protect your entire family and all your loved ones.

If you have ever worried about the safety of your family and loved ones in your absence, you need never be bothered by such worries again. The secrets of meta-cosmic projection contain the power that allows you to protect your family and loved ones even in your absence.

Man Uses Meta-Cosmic Projection to Protect His Family From Enemies

When I first heard Ronald D.'s story it sounded like a script for a horror movie. For two months Donald's entire family had been harrassed by their neighbors. Trash cans had been turned over on their front lawn, complaints had been phoned into the police departments concerning noisy parties that never took place, and two of their front windows had been broken three times. Ronald could give no reason for his neighbors' actions.

"I can't think of any reason for them to dislike us," he said. "None of it makes any sense. I don't even know for sure which neighbors are pulling the stunts. Can meta-cosmic projection protect us from enemies when we don't even know their names?"

I assured Ronald that the protection of meta-cosmic projection worked just as well for secret enemies as it did for known enemies. I also talked with him about psychic binoculars. He left determined to use his psychic binoculars, to discover why his neighbors acted as they did, and to use meta-cosmic projection to protect his family from those hostile acts.

Three weeks passed before I heard from Ronald again. He sounded like a new person.

"Everything has been going great," Ronald said. "With the help of psychic binoculars I discovered why our neighbors were out to get us. It was a misunderstanding about a rezoning petition for the neighborhood. Anyway, I used meta-cosmic projection to protect my home and family and no incidents have happened since I started using it."

I said I was glad to hear that things were so much better for Ronald and his family.

"Better is the understatement of the year," Ronald said. "Two of my neighbors, two men who are sort of leaders in the neighborhood, paid me a visit last night. They told me that some incorrect information had been circulated around the neighborhood and they had just found out it wasn't true. They also said they heard we had had some rotten luck with vandalism lately, but were sure we'd have no more such incidents. I'm sure we won't."

I congratulated Ronald on the successful resolution of his problem.

"Congratulations yourself," he said. "That meta-cosmic projection is the most powerful thing I've ever run across. You can bet my family will have the protection of meta-cosmic projection from here on out."

Meta-Cosmic Projection Saves a Man's Son

When Cecil G. asked to see me, he said it was a matter of life and death. He arrived in a state of anxiety and quickly told me his story.

"If you can't help me, I'm afraid my son Bobby is done for," Cecil said. "He informed on two dope pushers at his school and now a gang is trying to kill him. They beat him up pretty badly once. If a police car hadn't happened by, they might have killed him then. If he can't get some kind of really special protection, I'm afraid I'll lose him. If I only knew who the gang members are, the police could pick them up." He paused, then asked, "Can you help me to help my son?"

Before Cecil G. left, he had a thorough understanding of psychic binoculars and the secrets of meta-cosmic projection. In just six days he phoned.

"The police got the guys who were after my son," Cecil said. "I protected Bobby with meta-cosmic projection and used my psychic binoculars to find out who the men were who were after him. I told the police I had a possible lead without telling them how I got it. The police kept an eye on the men and when they tried to jump Bobby again they arrested them on the spot. It all happened two days ago, and I just got word from the police that with Bobby's testimony and their criminal records, those men won't be on the streets again for quite a long time."

We talked for a few minutes, and before we said good-bye Cecil returned to the subject of meta-cosmic projection.

"I plan to use meta-cosmic projection regularly," said Cecil. "Those secrets are much too powerful to be used only on special occasions or for emergencies."

Cecil G. was right. The secrets of meta-cosmic projection belong in everyday life. They belong in your daily life and you can put them there today.

Meta-Cosmic Projection Can Make You a Tower of Strength

No matter what the situation, the secrets of meta-cosmic projection can provide you with the strength and protection necessary to see it through successfully. You and your loved ones need never be unprotected again. Everything you need to know about the protection of meta-cosmic projection is waiting for you in this chapter.

Woman Protects Her Family With Meta-Cosmic Projection

Sharon A. had been aware of meta-cosmic projection for about five months. She and a friend had taken one of my classes, and Sharon had been quite impressed with meta-cosmic projection.

It had been months since I had heard from Sharon and when I received a phone call from her I was pleasantly surprised.

"I just thought you might like to hear what happened last night," Sharon said. "My husband had to be out of town on business and I was really jumpy being alone with the kids. There have been two robberies in the neighborhood in the last three months.

"If it hadn't been for meta-cosmic projection, I would have been scared to stay in the house without my husband. Anyway, I protected our home and family with meta-cosmic projection and settled in for the night. About two in the morning my doorbell rang. It was the police. They showed me their ID's through the peephole in the front door. It turned out that they had caught a man trying to break into my house through a side window. They weren't even supposed to be near my house at that time, but there they were to arrest the would-be housebreaker."

I told Sharon how happy I was that she and her family had not been hurt.

"I know that doesn't surprise you," said Sharon. "You've known about meta-cosmic projection for years. I've always known it works, but after last night I *really* know it works. The secrets of meta-cosmic projection sure do work great for protection."

The same secrets of meta-cosmic projection that worked for Sharon A. can work just as well for you. You and your loved ones deserve the invincible protection of meta-cosmic projection, and you can provide that protection today.

Your Meta-Cosmic Projection Technique for Protection Against All Enemies

Select a quiet place where you are not likely to be disturbed.

1. Lie down or sit in a chair whose back is high enough to support your head. Close your eyes.

2. For approximately thirty seconds, focus all your attention on your breathing. Make no attempt to control your breath, but simply pay attention to the intake and outflow of your own breathing.

3. In your mind's eye see or imagine yourself and/or your loved ones.

4. Create a mental motion picture and see or imagine a shield of white light completely surrounding you and/or your loved ones. (If you wish to include a house or car in this invincible protection, simply see or imagine that house and/or car also surrounded by a shield of white light.)

5. Repeat the following words to yourself mentally. (The words may be changed, but the meaning must remain the same.) "I surround myself (and/or my loved ones; and/or my house and automobile) with the invincible protection of meta-cosmic projection. The limitless power of meta-cosmic projection creates a shield so strong that no enemy can penetrate its protection. I and/or my loved ones are completely safe from the negative thoughts and actions of all enemies."

6. Again see or imagine yourself and/or your loved ones surrounded by the shield of pure white light -- the shield of meta-cosmic projection.

THE POWER OF META-COSMIC PROJECTION

7. *Once more, for approximately thirty seconds, place your attention on the intake and outflow of your own breath.*

8. *Open your eyes and go about your daily life.*

With these secrets of meta-cosmic projection, you and your loved ones can be safe from the negative thoughts and actions of all enemies.

The secret meta-cosmic projection technique is yours today. Begin now to protect yourself and your loved ones with the invincible power of meta-cosmic projection.

9
WORK WONDERS IN YOUR LIFE:

Through the secrets of Meta-Cosmic Projection.

Emergency situations and serious illnesses are not the only sources of frustrations in daily life. True, a crisis can have a devastating effect on one's emotions and physical body. However, the so-called "small" annoyances of daily living can also affect one's life in a powerful way. Which of us can honestly say we have never had "one of those days" when everything seemed to go wrong? Thanks to the secrets of meta-cosmic projection you can now say goodbye to "those days" forever. You need never waste another day suffering the small annoyances that can frustrate every activity of your life. The secrets of meta-cosmic projection presented to you in this chapter can keep your life free from all annoyances.

Your Psychic Binoculars Can Find a Needle in a Haystack

If you have never spent a half hour or longer looking for lost or misplaced keys, eyeglasses, pocketbooks, briefcases, screwdrivers, books, receipts, or the shoes you took off last night, you are indeed an unusual person. Most of us have at one time or another wasted minutes and even hours growing more and more annoyed as we searched for a lost or misplaced article we have put away for safe keeping.

Your psychic binoculars can help you find those lost or misplaced items as easily as one, two, three.

Using Her Psychic Binoculars, Woman Never Loses Anything

When I first met Ginny N. she was extremely annoyed with herself.

"Can you believe this?" asked Ginny. "I came to ask you what I can do about always losing things, and somewhere between my car and this office I've lost my car keys. I really need a method to help me stop losing or misplacing things. Do you have one you can teach me?"

What an opening for the response — "Do I have a technique for you!" Instead of making that response, however, I smiled and suggested that I demonstrate my method to her by finding her lost keys.

With the help of my psychic binoculars, I located Ginny's car keys near a water fountain in the hall. The entire process took less than five minutes.

"Wow!" said Ginny. "That's a technique I really need. Teach me to use my psychic binoculars."

We talked for about an hour and when Ginny left, she felt confident that she could use her psychic binoculars to find any item she might lose or misplace.

Two weeks passed before Ginny N. paid her second visit.

"You are looking at the new Sherlock Holmes in the field of lost articles!" Ginny said with a smile. "During these last two weeks, I've found things I had forgotten I lost. Psychic binoculars are terrific! My neighbors can't believe the way I've been finding things lost or misplaced. In fact, many of them have asked me to find articles they have lost."

Ginny grinned and her eyes reflected the pride evident in her voice. "I'm not ready to go into the lost and found business for my neighbors, but I did tell them about psychic binoculars. Every one of them wants to learn to use their psychic binoculars as soon as possible."

Ginny and I talked for a half hour. She left determined to teach her friends what she had learned about psychic binoculars.

"Thanks to my psychic binoculars, I'll never have to worry about losing anything. With my psychic binoculars, lost articles are so easy to find it's not even fair to say they were ever really lost. In fact, I don't ever expect to lose anything again."

Your Psychic Binocular Technique for Finding Lost Articles

This ultimately powerful technique should be used for one article at a time. Sets of things such as car keys, credit cards, and shoes are considered as single articles for the purpose of this technique.

1. Sit in a relaxed position. If your situation does not allow you to be seated, stand and relax as much as possible. Close your eyes.

2. For approximately thirty seconds, focus all your attention on your breathing. Make no attempt to control your breathing, simply give your attention to the intake and outflow of your breath.

3. In your mind's eye see or imagine the article you want to locate.

4. Now let your mind's eye "step back" and see or imagine the article you want to locate in its present surroundings. Make a mental note of these surroundings and the article's position in relationship to those surroundings.

5. For approximately thirty seconds, again give your attention to your breath without any attempt to control your breathing.

6. Open your eyes and reclaim the lost article using the picture of it and its surroundings presented to you by your psychic binoculars in step number four.

7. Open your eyes, and using the picture of the article and its surroundings presented to you by your psychic binoculars in step number four, proceed to the location you have seen and reclaim your article.

Traffic Problems Dissolve Before the Power of Your Psychic Binoculars

If you have never been vexed by traffic problems, you are indeed an unusual individual. If you have somehow escaped sitting in your car on a packed expressway and inching your way to your destination at less than a snail's pace, you are most fortunate and most unique. The majority of people in every industrialized society have known the annoyance of traffic tie-ups and other traffic problems. Those traffic tie-ups and other traffic problems melt away when viewed through the power of your psychic binoculars. You need never spend another wasted minute annoyed by traffic back-ups or other traffic problems. The power of your psychic binoculars can see you through to your destination without exasperating delays or other traffic annoyances. You need only use the powerful techniques presented to you in this chapter to make all traffic problems in your life a thing of the past.

Your Miraculous Psychic Shield Protects You Against Traffic Accidents

Traffic problems can be a terrible annoyance, but traffic accidents frequently result in serious physical injury and even death. Through the miraculous secrets of your psychic shield you can protect yourself and your loved ones against traffic accidents. Don't spend another day without the impenetrable protection of your psychic shield. Each step you need to follow in order to place this impenetrable psychic shield around those you love is presented to you in this chapter.

Woman Uses Her Psychic Binoculars to Breeze Through the Heaviest Traffic

It took a summer day with temperatures in the nineties, an hour and a half spent inching along a packed expressway, and an over-heated radiator to move Vivian R. to seek information about her psychic binoculars.

"I don't ever want to spend another ten minutes, let alone an hour and a half, tied up in traffic," said Vivian. "A couple of my friends have mentioned to me a method you taught them that keeps them out of traffic jams. I want to learn that technique."

Vivian and I talked for an hour or so and she left confident that she could use her psychic binoculars to keep her out of traffic tie-ups.

An entire month passed before I heard from Vivian again.

"I waited to call you until I could be sure the results I've gotten through my psychic binoculars are not just coincidence," Vivian said. "I started using the technique the same day I learned it. It's fantastic! I haven't been in one traffic tie-up since I started using my psychic binoculars to avoid traffic jams. The technique works like magic. I'm only sorry I didn't learn it sooner. No more traffic problems for me now that I know how to use my psychic binoculars."

What Vivian R. discovered is waiting for you in this chapter. The secret psychic binocular technique that allows you to breeze through the heaviest traffic is yours today. Begin now to put it to work in your life.

Psychic Shield Protects Man From Six-Car Pile-Up

Donald W. learned to use his psychic shield three months before he realized its power fully. Three months after Donald started to use his psychic shield on a daily basis, he witnessed and miraculously escaped involvement in, a mangled six-car pile-up. The excitement was evident in Donald's voice when he called to tell me about the incident.

"Even though I know how powerful the psychic shield is, seeing it in action is a real eye-opener," Donald said with conviction. "Logically my car and family should have been demolished. We were right in the middle of the thing when it started. By all rights we should have been the squashed middle car in the pile-up. Instead, a space opened up to my right and without remembering getting over to it, suddenly my car was in the other lane untouched, and the car that had been behind me plowed into the two cars in front. Then three more cars rammed the rear of his car."

Donald paused a few seconds to catch his breath.

"It was really a mess. Seven people were hurt, and all of the six cars were totally wrecked. I'm sure it was through the force of my psychic shield that we missed that accident. Believe me, there is no other way we could have escaped that pile-up. I don't intend to ever let my family be without the protection of a psychic shield again."

You and your family can have the protection of a psychic

shield today. The identical technique used by Donald W. is waiting for you in this chapter. Begin now to surround yourself and your loved ones with the invincible protection of your psychic shield.

Your Miraculous Psychic Binocular Technique for Dissolving All Traffic Problems

This powerful technique should be used before you start for your destination. (If your immediate destination has not been decided, use your return home as your designated destination.)

1. *Sit in a relaxed position. Close your eyes.*
2. *For approximately thirty seconds, focus all your attention on your breathing without any attempt to control it.*
3. *In your mind's eye see or imagine yourself beginning your trip to your destination. See or imagine the roads as if you were looking through the windshield of the car. See or imagine light and freely moving traffic in front of you. See or imagine your car moving freely without any delays. If the route you will travel has traffic lights on it, see or imagine each of these lights as green.*
4. *In your mind's eye see or imagine yourself arriving at your destination with time to spare.*
5. *For approximately thirty seconds, again focus all your attention on your breathing without attempting to control it.*
6. *Open your eyes and go about your daily life.*

If your trip involves several destinations, one following the other as in a shopping trip, you may include each destination in step three as if making one trip with several stops. You may also include your arrival at each destination in step four.

Any number of intervening destinations may be included in one performance of this powerful psychic binocular technique, as long as those intervening destinations are included in one day's travel. Each day's travel must be dealt with in order to obtain maximum effectiveness.

Your Miraculous Psychic Shield Technique for Encircling Yourself and Your Loved Ones With an Impenetrable Psychic Force Against Traffic Accidents

The use of this miraculous psychic shield technique once a day is sufficient to surround you and your loved ones with an impenetrable protection against traffic accidents.

1. Sit in a relaxed position. Close your eyes.

2. For approximately thirty seconds, focus all your attention on your breathing without any attempt to control your breath.

3. In your mind's eye see or imagine yourself and your car surrounded and enclosed by a bubble of white light.

4. In your mind's eye see or imagine your loved ones and their cars surrounded and enclosed in a bubble of white light.

5. Extend this impenetrable protection of your psychic shield to yourself and your loved ones in any car or motor vehicle in which any of you might ride, by seeing or imagining in your mind's eye a bubble of white light surrounding and enclosing you as a group. Now in your mind's eye see or imagine a bubble of dark blue light enclosing you, your loved ones, and the white bubble of light which surrounds you as a group.

6. For approximately thirty seconds, focus all your attention again on the intake and outflow of your breath without any attempt to control your breathing.

7. Open your eyes and go about your daily life.

You now have the miraculous secret techniques that will allow you to make lost articles a thing of the past, allow you to breeze through the heaviest traffic, and make it possible for you to surround yourself and your loved ones with an impenetrable protection against traffic accidents. Begin this very moment to use the miraculous secrets of meta-cosmic projection to work these wonders in *your* everyday life.

10
COMMUNICATE WITH OTHERS:

Through the inspiration of Meta-Cosmic Projection.

You and I most likely agree wholeheartedly that communication is of extreme importance to all mankind. Few people, if any, would choose to be cut off from meaningful contact with their friends and loved ones. Unfortunately, there are times in everyone's life when the communication one longs for seems unattainable. When hundreds, or even thousands of miles separate friend from friend and loved one from loved one, a telephone call or a letter can be a welcomed experience.

If you have ever sat and waited for a phone call or a letter you hoped would come, you most likely know what it is to feel helpless. By using the secrets of meta-cosmic projection presented to you in this chapter, you need never feel or be helpless in such a situation again. The miraculous force of meta-cosmic projection can put you in contact with a friend or loved one when you want that contact to take place. You need never waste another minute hoping a friend will call or visit. You need never spend another minute wondering why a loved one has not contacted you. The secrets of meta-cosmic projection are available to you right now, and allow you this very day to reach the people you seek to contact.

Woman Reestablishes Old Ties Through the Secrets of Meta-Cosmic Projection

The story Lilly D. told me was not a happy one. For all its unpleasantness, however, it was a story I had heard many times. The people change, but the circumstances in the stories are all too similar.

"I haven't heard from my sister in years," Lilly told me. "We quarrelled over some stupid thing I can't even remember now. Gail, that's my sister, was supposed to move out of state two days after the day of our argument."

Lilly paused and took a deep breath.

"Well, she moved all right. She never sent me her address, or her phone number. She refused to accept my calls at her job and the letters I sent to her at work were returned unopened.

"This has been going on for over two years. I know it must sound stupid to you, but it's deadly serious to me. Neither of us has another living relative and being cut off from Gail like this over some stupid argument is just killing me. I thought about just showing up at her company, but I don't want to cause her any trouble at work. If I knew how she'd react, it would be different, but for all I know, she could refuse even to recognize me.

"Can any of the techniques you teach people, help me get back in touch with my sister? I'm willing to try just about anything," Lilly said with resignation.

I assured Lilly that the secrets of meta-cosmic projection could very promptly put her back in touch with her sister. Lilly listened attentively as I explained the use of the meta-cosmic microphone to her.

"She's refused to hear anything else," said Lilly D. "I'm willing to try anything, including a meta-cosmic microphone."

Two weeks later, Lilly D. and a tall blonde woman walked into my office. "I'd like to introduce my sister, Gail D.," Lilly said.

I can't say I was surprised. I've seen the meta-cosmic microphone work too often and too well to be surprised by its repeated success.

As Lilly's story unfolded, I learned that Gail had telephoned three days after Lilly started using her meta-cosmic microphone. After a half hour of excited conversation, complete with tears and apologies on both sides, it was decided that Gail would pay Lilly a visit. When I met Gail, she and Lilly had been enjoying each other's company for five days.

"It's really great being back together again," said Lilly. "We both want to thank you for the secrets of meta-cosmic projection. That meta-cosmic microphone is absolutely terrific."

Six months ago Lilly D. called to say she was going to spend her vacation in St. Louis visiting her sister. They write regularly and talk to each other on the phone at least once every two weeks. Lilly's voice was excited as she spoke.

"Thanks to the secrets of meta-cosmic projection, I have a family again."

The Secrets of Meta-Cosmic Projection Can Bring You That Important Phone Call

Most people in our society consider the telephone a necessity rather than a luxury. In addition to casual conversations, many business deals are worked out and closed using the telephone as the instrument of communication. If you're like most people, you know what it is to wait for "that important phone call." Watched telephones in such situations are very similar to watched pots, they neither boil nor ring.

Thanks to the secrets of meta-cosmic projection, you never need to wait for an important phone call again. Using the miraculous force of meta-cosmic projection, you control your business dealings completely. If a phone call is what you need to close your deal, that phone call is yours, when you want it, and from the person you want to place the call. The secrets of meta-cosmic projection leave nothing to chance. Armed with these awesome secrets, presented to you in this chapter, you have the world at your beck and call. You need only decide what phone calls you want and from whom, and the secrets of meta-cosmic projection can do the rest.

The Secrets of Meta-Cosmic Projection Make it Possible for a Sales Manager to Contact His Salesmen

When Brian N. first visited me, he was a man beset by what he considered unsurmountable problems. Brian had been a sales manager for more than seven years. During that time he had tried many different methods to get his salesmen to phone in at regular intervals. The methods had ranged from incentives to threats. Despite all Brian's efforts, salesmen did not call in regularly and because of this his company missed many sales it might otherwise have consummated.

"I don't know what to do about it," Brian said. "It seems like I've tried everything. If you have a way to get those guys to call in regularly, I'd sure like to learn it."

I explained the meta-cosmic projection technique that I knew would work for Brian. He left with a firm resolve to give it a try.

Three weeks later Brian paid another visit. His face wore the expression of an adult who had just found out that Santa Claus really does exist.

"That meta-cosmic projection technique is absolutely fantastic," Brian said. "It's done what I couldn't do with incentives or threats. More than that, it did it in a week, when I'd tried everything I could think of for years and failed. Every one of my sales people now calls in regularly. I plan to use meta-cosmic projection a lot in my life. I just wish I had known about it sooner."

The secrets of meta-cosmic projection are yours now. The miraculous meta-cosmic projection techniques outlined for you in this chapter can completely solve your communication problems.

Woman Uses Meta-Cosmic Microphone to Reach Her Family by Telephone

Mary J.'s husband and children shared a common interest. Bob J. and the two sons, Jim and Roy, have been avid cave explorers since the boys were six and seven years old. As teenagers, the young men and their father spent, on an average, two weekends a month exploring near and distant caves.

"I'm used to their hobby," said Mary. "The thing that gets me is that it's just impossible to contact them when they're in the field. Maybe I won't ever need to reach them in an emergency, but what if I do? They camp by the caves they explore and they may or may not call me while they're out of town. Usually the only possible way I have to reach them is through some small general store, where they may or may not stop for supplies or a cold drink. I tried reaching them that way once before about three years ago. Bob's mother was in the hospital and on the critical list."

Mary paused briefly before she continued. "It didn't work

though. They had already stopped at the store and no one knew where they were camped. When they got home, Bob's mother was dead. It was really terrible."

"Anyway, what I need is a way to get in touch with them in an emergency. Naturally I hope that emergencies never arise, but I'd like to be ready if one does come up."

We talked for forty minutes or so and I taught Mary J. how to use her meta-cosmic microphone.

"If this meta-cosmic microphone works the way you say it will, it has to be fantastic," said Mary. "In a way I hope I never have to find out, but it will be great to have the technique if it's needed."

Five months later Mary telephoned me.

"I just wanted to thank you for teaching me how to use my meta-cosmic microphone. It worked when I really needed it," Mary said. "Two weeks ago I needed to contact Bob. I called the general store in the area where he and the boys were camping. The owner of the store recognized Bob and the boys from my description, but said they had been in earlier that day and he didn't really expect them back. He had no idea of where they had camped.

"I decided to use the meta-cosmic microphone technique you taught me. After going through the exercise, I waited for about an hour and called the general store again. While I was on the phone with the owner, Bob and the boys walked into the store. Even though I believed meta-cosmic projection would work, I was really amazed. The owner got so excited he almost hung up on me."

Mary went on to explain that she was able to get an important message to Bob that resulted in the close of a profitable business deal for him.

"It's the biggest commission he ever made," Mary said. "Thank goodness for the meta-cosmic microphone. Without it

Bob would have missed the deal completely. He is now a staunch advocate of meta-cosmic projection."

Naturally I was happy for Mary and her husband's success, however, the story was not new to me. The meta-cosmic microphone has worked for countless thousands of people. It can also work just as well for you. Learn the secrets of meta-cosmic projection now so that the meta-cosmic microphone can work for you if and when you need it.

Your Meta-Cosmic Projection Telephone Technique

Perform this meta-cosmic projection technique no more than four times a day.

1. Sit in a relaxed position. Close your eyes.

2. For approximately thirty seconds, focus all your attention on the intake and outflow of your breath without making an attempt to control your breathing.

3. In your mind's eye see or imagine the person from whom you want to receive a phone call. See or imagine this individual using a telephone and dialing your phone number.

4. See or imagine yourself by your telephone. Hear or imagine your telephone ringing. See or imagine yourself picking up the receiver of your phone and hear or imagine yourself saying, "Hello."

5. Now hear or imagine the voice of the person from whom you want a phone call saying the following or similar words, "Hello. I just had to call you. How are things going?"

6. Hear or imagine your response to the person's voice by repeating the following or similar words in your own mind. "I'm really glad you called. I really wanted to talk with you." (The remainder of the conversation will just follow naturally. There is no need for you to go through any except this introduction conversation in order for the phone call to take place.)

7. For approximately thirty seconds, again focus all your attention on your breathing without making any attempt to control your breath.

8. Open your eyes and go about your daily life.

Meta-Cosmic Projection Can Bring Old Friends Back Into Your Life

Telephone communication is great, but face to face communication has it beaten by a mile. It's only natural that you and I would, in most cases, prefer to actually be in the company of our friends and loved ones rather than speak with them by telephone. Through the secrets of meta-cosmic projection you can renew old friendships in person. Even if your old friends have moved to another state, the secrets of meta-cosmic projection can bring those friends back into your life now.

Woman Uses Her Meta-Cosmic Microphone to Hold Her Own Class Reunion

Rose A. had left many old friends behind when she moved from the West Coast. Most of the friends Rose missed had grown up with her and they had shared many happy times together.

"I sure would like to see them again," said Rose. "It's been about three years since any of us got together. The trouble is we're all scattered to different states now. Can meta-cosmic projection bring any of them into my life again?"

During the hour we talked, I explained the secrets of the meta-cosmic microphone to Rose.

"It sounds great. If it works I'll probably wear it out," Rose said.

Three weeks later Rose was back in my office.

"I've met five old friends right here in town since I started using my meta-cosmic microphone," she said with a smile. "I went to high school with all of them and now we all live in different states.

"It's just fantastic the way they turned up here and we bumped into each other. It's as if I've been holding my own private class reunion. Believe me, I loved every minute of it. Meta-cosmic projection has my vote all the way."

Rose telephoned a week later to say she had "bumped into three more old classmates."

"I'm absolutely certain now that I can bring any friend back into my life with the secrets of meta-cosmic projection. This technique is positively terrific!"

The same fantastic meta-cosmic microphone technique used by Rose is available to you at this very moment. Don't spend another day just wanting to meet old friends again. Begin now to use the secrets of meta-cosmic projection and bring those friends back into your life now.

Your Meta-Cosmic Microphone Technique to Bring Old Friends Back Into Your Life

Use this Meta-Cosmic Microphone technique no more than four times a day.

1. Sit in a relaxed position. Close your eyes.

2. For approximately thirty seconds, focus all your attention on the intake and outflow of your breath without making any attempt to control your breathing.

3. In your mind's eye see or imagine the person (or people, up to four individuals) you want to meet. Form as clear a picture of the person (or people) as you call to mind.

4. See or imagine yourself in a situation where you meet this person (or people) without a prearranged time of meeting between you.

5. Hear or imagine this person (or people) saying the fol-

lowing or similar words. "It's really good to see you again. Imagine us just bumping into each other like this!"

6. Hear or imagine your response to this individual using the following or similar words. "It's great to see you. I've thought of you often. What are you doing in town?"

7. Again for approximately thirty seconds, focus all your attention on the intake and outflow of your breath. Make no attempt to control your breathing.

8. Open your eyes and go about your daily life.

Through the Secrets of Meta-Cosmic Projection You Can Solve All Your Communication Problems

The secrets of meta-cosmic projection presented to you in this chapter give you the power to solve all your communication problems. Don't waste another minute hoping someone will call, or you will find a certain person in your life again. Begin today to use the secrets of meta-cosmic projection to get the calls you want when you want them, and bring old friends back into your life now.

11

META-COSMIC PROTECTION FOR YOU AND YOUR LOVED ONES:

At home, work and play.

In the society in which we live, we hear a lot of talk about protection and insurance. The secrets of meta-cosmic projection can protect you with an impenetrable meta-psychic shield. There is no force on earth that can equal the miraculous force of your meta-psychic shield or the protection it gives you.

The Secrets of Meta-Cosmic Projection Can Protect Your Home from Burglary and Fire

Despite the rising crime rate in our country and the dangers lawbreakers place around us, the ultimate power of meta-cosmic projection can surround you with a protection no force can penetrate. The miraculous power of meta-cosmic projection is far stronger than any burglars, and can also protect your home from the dangers of fire. The secrets of meta-cosmic projection given to you in this chapter allow you to protect your home and loved ones from this moment on, from burglars and fire. Give your home and family the protection of your meta-psychic shield today.

Man Protects His Home from Burglars Through the Secrets of Meta-Cosmic Projection

A series of burglaries that concentrated on single family homes and apartment complexes led Robert L. to seek my help.

"I have plenty of home insurance," said Robert. "I'd rather not have a need to turn in a claim if it can be prevented. I'm a firm believer in prevention, and from what I've heard about meta-cosmic projection, it's very big in that area."

Robert went on to explain that he wanted to learn how to surround his home and family with the protection of meta-cosmic projection.

We talked for quite a while and Robert left with a firm resolve to make his home safe from burglary by using the secrets of meta-cosmic projection.

Three months went by before I heard from him again. "That meta-cosmic projection really works," said Robert. "In fact it works so well I was beginning to feel kind of strange. Burglars have hit the houses on both sides of us. They also broke into four homes across the street. Neighbors were beginning to look at us out of the corners of their eyes.

"I honestly felt better when two detectives doing part of the police investigation discovered that burglars had actually tried to break into my home through a side window." Robert paused very briefly. "The bar they used to try to open the window snapped. The burglars just left it in the ground and decided to go elsewhere.

"I sure am glad that I learned to use meta-cosmic projection. It's better than any protection technique I've ever heard anyone talk about. In fact, I can't imagine anything that could possibly top it."

Man Uses Meta-Cosmic Projection to Protect His Home from Fire

When Dan S. asked to learn the secrets of meta-cosmic projection, he couldn't think of anything in particular he wanted to use them for, but had many plans for them in general. "I'm not really afraid of burglars," Dan said. "The apartments I live in have a very good security system. The only thing that's given the apartment complex any trouble has been two fires. Both of them did quite a bit of damage. No one was seriously injured, but the apartments where the fires started were completely gutted. In addition, the apartments on either side of those apartments were also gutted. Maybe I'd be wise to use meta-cosmic projection against fires."

I respected Dan's wishes and concentrated on teaching him a meta-cosmic projection technique to protect his home against fires. A full six months passed before I heard from Dan again. His voice sounded excited as it came from the telephone receiver.

"Did you see the news last night?" said Dan. Before I could say "no" he continued. "There was a fire at my apartment complex late yesterday afternoon. Five apartments were gutted. Somehow the sprinkler systems didn't work in any of them."

"Also," Dan placed more emphasis in his words, "my apartment was right in the middle of the group that was wiped out. The fire skipped right over it. I didn't even get any smoke damage. The firemen said it was just a freak happening, but I know better than that. The protection of meta-cosmic projection is what saved my apartment from that fire. I sure am glad I learned how to use it. Meta-cosmic projection is the best thing I've discovered. It's just terrific."

The same meta-cosmic projection techniques that protected Robert L.'s home from burglars and Dan S.'s home from fire are yours to use today. The same impenetrable force that protected the homes of these men, and countless others, is available to you right now. The secrets of meta-cosmic projection presented to you in this chapter can provide you with a protection stronger than any force the world can mount against you.

Your Meta-Psychic Shield Technique for Complete Protection of Your Home

Use this meta-psychic shield technique at least once a day, and no more than three times a day.

1. Sit in a relaxed position. Close your eyes.

2. For approximately thirty seconds, focus all your attention on the intake and outflow of your breath. Make no attempt to control your breathing.

3. In your mind's eye see or imagine your home as it looks from the outside. See or imagine a bubble of pure white light completely surrounding your home and enclosing it within a circle of light.

4. Now in your mind's eye see or imagine your home as it looks from the inside. (You can imagine or see a complete view of the inside of your home as if you were looking from a high place, or you can see or imagine room by room individually.) See or imagine a pure white light filling every room in your home.

5. In your mind repeat the following words, or use words

that convey the same meaning. "My home, and all within it, is protected by the impenetrable force of my meta-psychic shield. No harm can come to my home, or those within it, either from within or without. The miraculous power of my meta-psychic shield makes my home the perfect sanctuary against all forces of harm."

6. Again for thirty seconds, focus all your attention on the intake and outflow of your breath. Make no attempt to control your breathing.

7. Open your eyes and go about your daily life.

The Secrets of Meta-Cosmic Projection Can Protect You in Hazardous Working Conditions

Chances are that one or more of your loved ones works in hazardous conditions regularly or intermittently. Perhaps you yourself find it necessary to work in hazardous conditions. Even if you or your loved ones work in hazardous conditions only once or twice a year, you need protection. The secrets of meta-cosmic projection can keep you completely safe even in the most hazardous working conditions. Don't deny yourself or your loved ones this miraculous protection one more day. Start now to put the secrets of meta-cosmic projection to work in your life.

Man Uses His Meta-Psychic Shield to Remain Accident-Free at Work

Tim R. visited me with one thing in mind. He wanted to learn a technique that would keep him accident-free in his hazardous job. For six years Tim had worked on a production line in a major factory. The company experienced a number of accidents each month due to the hazardous nature of the work. Tim had been involved in one accident in which his left hand was badly cut and required fourteen stitches to close the laceration. He was determined not to experience a repetition of that accident.

"I need any protection I can get," Tim said. "My job is really dangerous, and if you have a special technique that could protect me from accidents, I sure would like to learn it."

Tim listened attentively while I explained the use of the meta-psychic shield to protect him from accidents at work. Before he left he said he planned to use the meta-psychic shield technique every day.

Eight months later I received a phone call from Tim.

"Just thought you might like to know that the meta-psychic shield has saved my neck twice in the last eight months. Twice I should have been badly hurt and got away without a scratch. The guys at work have tagged me with the name Lucky. I told them that luck doesn't have a thing to do with it. I also told a couple of them, the ones I know real well, about the meta-psychic shield. I even taught them how to use it.

"Thanks a lot for letting me in on that thing. That meta-psychic shield is something else. It's absolutely fantastic!"

Your Meta-Psychic Shield Technique to Protect You and Your Loved Ones in Hazardous Working Conditions

Use this meta-psychic shield technique at least once every working day, and no more than twice on any working day.

1. Sit in a relaxed position. Close your eyes.

2. For approximately thirty seconds, focus all your attention on your breathing. Make no attempt to control your breath.

3. In your mind's eye see or imagine yourself (and/or your loved ones) at work. See or imagine a bubble of pure white light surrounding you (and/or your loved ones) and encircling you completely.

4. For approximately thirty seconds, again focus all your

attention on your breathing. Make no attempt to control your breath.

5. *Open your eyes and go about your daily life.*

Your Meta-Psychic Shield Can Also Surround Your Vacation Activities

Vacations need the protection of your meta-psychic shield too. Frequently people take more chances on vacation than they do in their everyday life. Those extra chances can range from extra time on the roads or in the skies traveling, to hours spent swimming, or hours spent zooming down snow-covered slopes. All the activities that mark the average vacation tend to be more risky than the activities of everyday life.

Woman Uses the Meta-Psychic Shield to Protect Her Family on a Skiing Trip

Skiing trips were not new to Dottie F. and her family. The entire family had taken a skiing vacation together twice a year for three years. Unfortunately, those vacations had been marked by a series of skiing accidents resulting in fractures and concussions.

"I'd like this year to be different," Dottie said at our first meeting. "It seems like my sons and husband take turns getting hurt each year. I've heard of that meta-psychic shield you teach people to use, and I'd like you to teach me to use it for myself and my family."

After forty minutes, Dottie felt confident that she could protect herself and her family during their vacations. She left with a smile and the words, "No more fractures. How wonderful that will be! A skiing trip without broken bones."

One month later I received Dottie's report. "It was one great vacation," Dottie said. "Not one broken bone, not one dislocated knee cap, not even a serious bruise. It was just wonderful."

Dottie went on raving about her vacation for a full twenty minutes before she mentioned hanging up.

"I'd better let you go," she said. "I want you to know, though, that the meta-psychic shield is the greatest thing to come down the slopes. I'm absolutely sold on it."

I can't blame Dottie for being excited about how well the meta-psychic shield works. It is fantastic. You need only use the secrets of meta-cosmic projection presented to you in this chapter in order to discover why Dottie, I, and countless others are sold on the meta-psychic shield and meta-cosmic projection in general.

Your Meta-Psychic Shield Technique to Protect You and Your Family in All Vacation Activities

Use this meta-psychic shield technique the day before you start your vacation. It is not necessary to use the techniques daily during your vacation.

1. Sit in a relaxed position. Close your eyes.

2. For approximately thirty seconds, focus all your attention on your breathing. Make no attempt to control your breath.

3. In your mind's eye see or imagine yourself and your family. Now see or imagine yourself and your family surrounded by a bubble of pure white light which encircles you totally.

4. See or imagine a calendar and focus your attention on the dates of your family vacation. Now see or imagine those dates completely surrounded by a bubble of pure white light.

5. Once again see or imagine yourself and your family surrounded by a bubble of pure white light.

6. For approximately thirty seconds, again focus all your attention on your breathing. Make no attempt to control your breath.

7. Open your eyes and go about your daily life.

The wonderful and miraculous secrets of meta-cosmic projection given to you in this chapter can protect you, your friends, and your loved ones, at home, at work, and at play. The protection provided by the secrets of meta-cosmic projection cannot be equaled. Don't allow yourself or those you love to go without this ultimate protection another day. Begin now to put the secrets of meta-cosmic projection to work in your life.

12

THE META-COSMIC DIVINING ROD:

The power that points to the answers in your life.

It's only natural that when you feel a need for guidance you want it *now* — not next week. If you have ever tried to get an appointment with a psychologist or psychotherapist in a hurry, you most likely found that the next available appointment open was anywhere from two weeks to four weeks away. That two to four-week wait can be a most uncomfortable period for anyone experiencing the pain of anxiety and stress. Thanks to the secrets of meta-cosmic projection presented to you in this chapter, you can be your own best counselor. The secrets of meta-cosmic projection are on call 24 hours a day, and you need never wait for two weeks or even two hours to gain the inner guidance you seek.

It is an unfortunate fact that in this country many people

visit psychotherapists regularly for a period of many years. The time and monetary costs for these visits can be phenomenal. The emotional costs can be even more severe if the individual client or patient is not progressing toward a position where he or she can depend on his or her own inner guidance. You receive no favor from anyone who teaches you to depend, not on yourself, but on another person. One of the greatest gifts one can give to another is to teach that person to stand on his or her own two feet, and recognize the sound of his or her own inner guidance. The secrets of meta-cosmic projection that are in this chapter can enable you to reach and recognize the sound of your own inner voice.

Strange as it may seem to you, the majority of people have never learned to search for their own inner voice, let alone listen to it. The secrets of meta-cosmic projection can give you the power to recognize, hear, and follow your own inner guidance. You need only follow the limitless meta-cosmic projection technique.

Man Uses Meta-Cosmic Projection and Stops a Six-Year Psychotherapy Habit

Robert M. paid me a visit the day after his weekly therapy session.

"I've been in therapy for six years and I still can't see the day when my therapist will say I don't need it any longer," Robert said. "I'm really tired of therapy. I've had four different therapists in six years and with each new therapist it seems like I went all the way back to the beginning."

Robert talked for a half hour discussing his feelings about his dependence on others for guidance.

"I'm just plain tired of always waiting to find out what someone else thinks I should do in a situation. It's about time I started listening to myself. Six years of therapy haven't taught me how to do that. Can you teach me to hear myself through meta-cosmic projection? I'm willing to do all it will take in order to be my own counselor."

After assuring Robert that the secrets of meta-cosmic projection could indeed teach him to hear his own inner guidance, I presented him with the secret technique that could make him his own best counselor.

"It sounds good," said Robert. "I'll start using it today. If it can help me break a six-year psychotherapy habit, it can do anything."

Three weeks later Robert M. returned for another visit.

"I've finally kicked the habit," he said. "I went to my last psychotherapy session two weeks ago." The warm smile on Robert's face reflected the pride he felt in himself.

"Before I learned that meta-cosmic projection technique, I would have been in a panic if I missed even one session. Now I've announced my resignation from therapy and I never felt better," Robert said. "That technique is absolutely fantastic."

That same fantastic meta-cosmic projection technique is waiting for you in the following pages. It's time that you too become your own best counselor.

Young Couple Uses Meta-Cosmic Projection to Put Them in Touch With Their Own Inner Guidance

Ted and Sandra T. had been married for four years when they visited me. During that time Sandra had worked and contributed her income to enable Ted to return to college for a master's degree in business. Shortly after Ted graduated, trouble broke out in the young couple's home.

"Ever since he received his master's degree, he acts like he's too good for our way of life and our old friends," Sandra said. "I just don't understand how one person can change so much and in such a short period of time. He's not the same person I married."

"That's ridiculous!" Ted responded. "I've explained a

hundred times to you that I have more responsibilities at work now. I just don't have the same amount of time to socialize. Besides, I've met a lot of new people and I'd like to fit them into our social life too. If you'd give yourself half a chance you'd like these people. I have to work with them and I'd like to get to know them better."

"*You* get to know them better," said Sandra. "Maybe Ken and Judy are right. Maybe we should get a divorce."

I interrupted the ongoing battle long enough to ask why they had come to see me.

"We thought you might be able to advise us," Sandra said. "Do you think we should just go our separate ways?"

In no less than two minutes I made it very clear to both Sandra and Ted that I didn't tell people what they should do. I offered to teach them a secret meta-cosmic projection technique that would allow them to get in touch with their own true feelings.

"That sounds good to me," said Ted. "How do we start?"

Sandra agreed that the technique sounded pretty good if it would really work. For forty minutes we discussed the meta-cosmic projection technique that would allow Ted and Sandra to hear their own inner voice. The young couple left vowing to use the technique daily.

One month later Ted and Sandra paid me a second visit.

"That technique really works," said Ted. "It allowed us to see that we were both wrong in some ways and both right in other ways. It really helped us get our heads together. I know I speak for Sandra too when I say we're happier than we've ever been since we learned about meta-cosmic projection."

"Ted is right," said Sandra. "That technique is terrific. Our whole life has just fallen into place. Once we could hear ourselves, we could hear each other." She smiled at her husband

and said, "We really are happy again. Thanks for the meta-cosmic projection."

Meta-Cosmic Projection Can Help You Choose the Best of Two Great Opportunities

You and I know that it's often difficult for people to make a choice when two or more great opportunities are offered to them. In fact, one very successful game show on TV operates on this principle. Contestants are often asked to choose between a possible trip to Europe and a possible new car. Once they make a decision the host often presents them with another great opportunity so they are right back to choosing again. The tension and suspense created by this situation has kept this show on TV for four nights a week in many cities, and has placed the show at the top of listings in its category.

The tension and stress that makes this game show a terrific success can bring many uncomfortable moments to ordinary life. The secrets of meta-cosmic projection can do away with that anxiety and all the uncomfortable feelings that accompany it. With the meta-cosmic projection technique given in this chapter you can easily choose between or among great opportunities presented to you and consistently choose the best one.

Man Uses Meta-Cosmic Projection to Choose the Right Job Opportunity

Some people would consider the situation that faced Sid W. a blessing rather than a problem. The anxiety experienced by Sid, however, made the choice a very real problem for him.

Sid was faced with two excellent job offers. The favorable

aspects surrounding each job opportunity far outweighed any negative aspects seen by Sid.

"Both offers promise a great future," said Sid. "The money and benefits involved in each are just about equal. I honestly don't know which job to accept."

The intensity and emphasis in Sid's voice underlined the reality of the problem he faced.

"I've gotten unsolicited advice from two close friends. Neither of the people who offered opinions agreed with each other. I could ask your advice, but I already know that you don't make people's decisions for them." Sid raised one eyebrow. "I'd like you to teach me one of those meta-cosmic projection techniques so I can make the best decision myself. How about it? Will you teach me?"

Five months passed before I heard from Sid again. "I waited to contact you so I could see if my decision was the best one," Sid said. "I guess I really didn't have to wait as long as I did to consider my decision a good one, but, in a way, I'm glad I did.

"I've already received a promotion, an unbelievable happenstance for an employee of less than six months, and the future looks even brighter. The job I could have chosen, but didn't, was phased out two months afterward. If it hadn't been for that meta-cosmic projection technique you taught me, that would have been me being phased out. I was leaning toward that job before I learned how to listen to my own inner guidance. I want you to know that I'm sold 100 percent on meta-cosmic projection."

Meta-Cosmic Projection Lets You Know When You're Right

Not everyone has to wait for months to know that the decision they made through meta-cosmic projection was correct. Some people have discovered in less than an hour that the secrets of meta-cosmic projection have put them in touch with their own inner guidance, and that that guidance is true.

Woman Follows the Inner Guidance of Meta-Cosmic Projection and Saves Her Daughter's Life

Edna D. had used the secrets of meta-cosmic projection for almost a year before she faced one of the most crucial decisions of her life. Three weeks after the incident I learned of the event.

"I had just hung up the phone after talking with my daughter. It hit me that something was wrong with her. I couldn't put my finger on it so I called her back." Edna paused briefly. "Gail, my daughter, insisted that everything was fine. When I hung the phone up again I still couldn't shake the feeling that something about her voice was wrong.

"I decided to use my own inner guidance and went through the meta-cosmic projection technique you taught me a long time ago. My inner guidance told me to get right over to my daughter's apartment. When I arrived, she didn't answer the door. I rang the bell for five minutes before I got the apartment manager to let me in. We found Gail unconscious in her bedroom. She'd taken an overdose of sleeping pills. I called an emergency squad and they got her to a hospital in time to save her life.

"When she could talk, she told me her boyfriend had found someone new and she decided she didn't want to live without him." Edna paused again and took a deep breath.

"She feels differently now. Now she's glad she wasn't successful. If it hadn't been for meta-cosmic projection, and following my inner guidance, Gail would most likely be dead. Boy, am I glad I learned that meta-cosmic projection technique. I owe my daughter's life to meta-cosmic projection."

The Secrets of Meta-Cosmic Projection and Inner Guidance Are Yours Now

The same miraculous meta-cosmic projection technique that has enabled so many people to hear and follow their own inner guidance are yours today. You need only follow the easy step-by-step technique presented for you here in order to have the benefits of your own inner guidance in your life now.

Your Meta-Cosmic Projection Technique That Can Provide You With Inner Guidance Today

Use this technique once a day for a full week, then use the technique whenever inner guidance is needed in a situation. Do not use the technique more than four times in one day.

1. Sit in a relaxed position. Close your eyes.

2. For approximately thirty seconds, focus all your attention on your breathing without attempting to control it.

3. In your mind and in your own words state the problem that faces you. (For example, "Two jobs have been offered to me. I want to choose the better of these two jobs. I want to choose the job that offers me the best future.")

4. In your own mind and in your own words state the alternatives open to you. (For example, "I can choose either job offer or I can look for another job offer, or I can stay on my present job.")

5. In your own mind and in your own words state the positive things which you see in each alternative. (For example, "If I stay where I am, I at least know what is expected of me and I also know my co-workers pretty well. If I choose job offer number one, I have a chance for rapid promotion and also receive excellent fringe benefits. If I choose job offer number two, I have a chance for promotion and relocation to the West Coast along with excellent fringe benefits. I would also be able to spend more time with my family and friends. If I seek an

THE META-COSMIC DIVINING ROD

entirely different job opportunity, I may find one even more to my liking.")

6. *In your own mind and in your own words state the negative things which you see in each alternative. (For example, "If I stay where I am, my chances for promotion are very slim. Besides, I sometimes get very bored doing the same things at work every day. If I choose job offer number one, I'd have to take on some job duties I know I won't like. The company is fairly new also, and has not really proven its ability to last through an economic crisis if it should arise. If I choose job offer number two, I may have to move to the West Coast before next year and my children will have to change schools in mid-term. My wife isn't sure she wants to live on the West Coast anyway and no one in the family is looking forward to saying goodbye to friends they've known all their lives. If I seek an entirely new job offer, I may never find one as good as the two I have now. It could also take a long time to get another off. The market is very tight."*)

7. *For approximately twenty seconds, focus all your attention on your breathing without attempting to control it.*

8. *In your own mind repeat the following words or use your own words to express the same meaning. "I am now stilling my mind and will hear the voice of my own inner guidance. The wisdom of my inner guidance already knows what is best for me and will now make this information known to my conscious mind."*

9. *Take one deep breath and listen to your own thoughts which flow from the voice of your inner guidance.*

10. *Again for approximately thirty seconds, focus all your attention on your breathing without attempting to control your breath.*

11. *Open your eyes and go about your daily life.*

The miraculous secrets of meta-cosmic projection can put the voice of your inner guidance within your reach today. Don't waste another hour suffering the pain of indecision. The miraculous meta-cosmic projection technique given to you in this chapter can make you your own best counselor.

13

BRING THE JOYOUS RESULTS YOU DESIRE:

Through the magic of Meta-Cosmic Projection.

If there is any one thing we have a great variety of in our country it is meetings. You can take your pick — social club meetings, civic organization meetings, meetings for neighborhood action, political meetings, professional group meetings, or business meetings. Whatever the occasion for the meeting you attend, chances are you find it necessary to attend one or more meetings a month. The secrets of meta-cosmic projection make it possible for you to be in complete control of each meeting you attend.

Most people have had the experience of attending a social or business meeting whose outcome was not what they wanted. Thanks to the secret meta-cosmic technique given to you in this chapter, you can completely control the outcome of meetings you attend. In fact, this technique allows you to decide the outcome of a meeting before that meeting ever begins.

Man Uses His Psychic Organizer and Meta-Cosmic Projection to Sell a Sales Idea to His Company

Greg M. had been a salesman for seven years when he visited me. Success was no stranger to Greg in his profession and his request was directly related to his work.

"I have an idea that will increase our sales tremendously," said Greg. "My only problem is the fact that our sales managers frown on just about every new idea. I learned that through bitter experience. The last idea I presented was all but laughed under the table. I'm not even sure I'd be willing to risk presenting my new idea without something extra going for me. I want that something extra to be one of those techniques you teach people."

Greg and I talked for a half hour concerning the way he wanted his idea to be accepted and acted upon. Then our conversation shifted to the use of the psychic organizer and meta-cosmic projection. When Greg left he was confident that he could completely control his upcoming business meeting and determine its outcome.

Ten days later Greg phoned.

"Everything went great," he said. "The meeting went exactly as I saw it with my psychic organizer. That meta-cosmic projection sure packs a wallop. When our district sales manager said he thought my idea was great, I almost cheered. It went so well, my idea is already being introduced in all our sales districts."

With the help of the meta-cosmic projection technique in

this chapter you can control your meetings just as effectively as Greg controlled the outcome of his sales meeting.

Man Uses Meta-Cosmic Projection to Close a Big Deal for His Company

Chances are that most if not all commercial real estate salesmen would agree that closing a deal can often be the most delicate part of their responsibilities. Daren T. certainly felt that way.

"The closings are the only part of my job that really trip me up," said Daren. "Right now I'm at the point of closing a very large commercial real estate deal, and I need all the help I can get so I won't lose the deal at the last minute."

In less than an hour Daren was convinced he would have no problem with his deal thanks to the secrets of meta-cosmic projection.

Two weeks later Daren was back in my office and obviously elated.

"My deal was finalized yesterday," Daren said. "It's the largest commission I've ever earned. Would you believe that the guy had actually decided against buying the property and didn't change his mind until yesterday morning. He doesn't know why he changed his mind, but all of a sudden the deal really looked great to him. He kiddingly asked me if I had cast a spell on him. I told him no, that I had only used some powerful magic on the deal itself. That meta-cosmic projection is the most powerful technique I've ever seen. It will be part of all my real estate deals from now on."

Daren T. had found, just as thousands before him, that the secrets of meta-cosmic projection can bring the desired end in business deals. That same meta-cosmic projection technique used by Daren T. is available to you this very minute. It can bring the ends you want in your business deals.

Woman Uses Her Psychic Organizer and Meta-Cosmic Projection to Become President of Her Woman's Club

Cynthia B. was a member of a woman's club that sponsored many activities for disadvantaged young people. Her visit to me was prompted by her club's gradual drift away from such activities.

"It may not be a big thing," Cynthia said, "but it's important to me. I want the club to start sponsoring young people's groups again. The president we've had for the last year has turned our meetings into plain old social gatherings. That can be a lot of fun, but our club was founded to help people, not to throw parties.

"I figure the only way to get the club back on the right road is to get myself elected president. That would be quite a job, however, since I'm not known as Miss Friendliness to other club members. In fact, many of them think I'm too serious.

"Can you teach me any technique I can use to get elected president? I really feel I can do a lot of good if I'm elected."

After Cynthia told me more about her plans for the club, we settled down to the meta-cosmic projection technique she could use to be elected president. The new club elections were to be held in a week and Cynthia left with a surety that she would win the post she wanted.

The day the elections were held. Cynthia phoned. "It worked. I'm the new club president." Cynthia's voice bubbled through the receiver. "I won unanimously. Everyone was surprised, but they all congratulated me."

I added my congratulations and Cynthia continued.

"I already have my committees set up to start the work

with young people again. I plan to use the same technique to ensure the success of our programs with those kids. Meta-cosmic projection and my psychic organizer are going to play a big role in the work of our club from here on out. Thanks a lot for the technique."

Cynthia's club has since sponsored some wonderful programs for disadvantaged young people. Each one has been a huge success.

Like Cynthia, you can have any office you want in social and civic organizations. You need only follow the meta-cosmic projection technique in this chapter and you can have the office you want now.

Man Uses His Psychic Organizer and Meta-Cosmic Projection to Become Captain of His Bowling Team

There are thousands of bowling teams in this country and chances are that you or someone you know is a member of one of those teams. Harry L. had been an avid bowler for fifteen years when he visited me concerning his bowling team.

"I'm a pretty good bowler, but lately my game has fallen off quite a bit," Harry said. "Just last week the guy who has been captain of our team for five years announced that he was moving out of state. This meant we'd have to choose a new captain."

Harry paused momentarily and a smile lit up his eyes.

"I'd like to be the new captain. If the team had decided to vote for one I'd probably have it in the bag. Instead, it was decided that the guy with the best combined score in three games next week will be the team captain."

Harry went on to explain that his score had gotten so bad he was afraid he couldn't win the contest to become captain of his team.

"I've heard that you can teach people how to get what they want. Would you teach me some kind of technique to improve my bowling and get me appointed captain?"

Harry learned to use his psychic organizer and meta-cosmic projection. He left with a promise to let me know how things turned out.

The day after the big game Harry phoned. "I made it!" he said. "I had the highest combined scores of the whole team. I am now the new team captain. Thanks an awful lot for teaching me how to use meta-cosmic projection and my psychic organizer. I intend to use that technique every time I bowl."

Harry had learned what thousands of others already know, that with the secrets of meta-cosmic projection and the psychic organizer, happy endings are never a problem. With the limitless power of the meta-cosmic projection technique, you can have the happy endings you want now.

Woman Uses the Secrets of Meta-Cosmic Projection to Win the Lead in a Play

When Karen C. phoned me she had already attained her happy ending. Karen called to tell me how well the meta-cosmic projection technique she had learned months before had worked for her.

"You know, I always knew the technique worked, but sometimes I forgot to use it," Karen said. "When my woman's club announced trials for the annual play, I decided that I wanted the lead role. I told a couple of my girlfriends and they nearly fell out of their chairs laughing. They just couldn't see me in any role in the play.

"I used the meta-cosmic projection technique you taught me four months ago — the one for happy endings. Boy, did it work! I was the third person to try out for the role. After I did the scene at the audition, they cancelled all other tryouts for the part. The eight others who had signed up for the part didn't even get mad. Instead, everyone congratulated me and said I had real acting talent. The whole thing is fantastic. That meta-cosmic projection really works great.

"If you get a chance you'll have to come see the play."

Unfortunately, I didn't get to see the play. I did hear a lot about it, however, and everyone agreed that Karen was terrific in her part.

You may never want the lead in a play, but the secrets of meta-cosmic projection stand ready to bring the result you want in any area.

Your Psychic Organizer Technique of Meta-Cosmic Projection That Allows You to Write Your Own Happy Endings

When you use this technique to bring about the result you want in a situation, use the technique twice daily.

1. Sit in a comfortable position. Close your eyes.

2. For approximately thirty seconds, focus all your attention on your breathing without attempting to control your breath.

3. In your mind's eye see or imagine yourself in the situation you desire. In your mind's eye see all the people who would be involved in this situation standing with you.

4. See or imagine these people going through the actions necessary to bring about the end you want. Hear everyone concerned saying the words you want to hear to bring about the result you want.

5. See and hear or imagine in your mind's eye saying and doing the things necessary to bring about the end result you want.

6. In your own mind repeat the following words or choose your own words as long as you retain the overall meaning. "My *psychic organizer, aspect of my higher mind, has separated and organized all circumstances necessary to bring the end result I want into reality. The happy ending I want in this situation exists now, and I am now ever more conscious of its existence."*

7. Again for approximately thirty seconds, focus all your attention on your breathing without any attempt to control your breath.

8. Open your eyes and go about your daily life.

With the secrets of meta-cosmic projection you can control the outcome of every situation that involves you. Begin to use the secrets of meta-cosmic projection and your psychic organizer and write your own happy ending today.

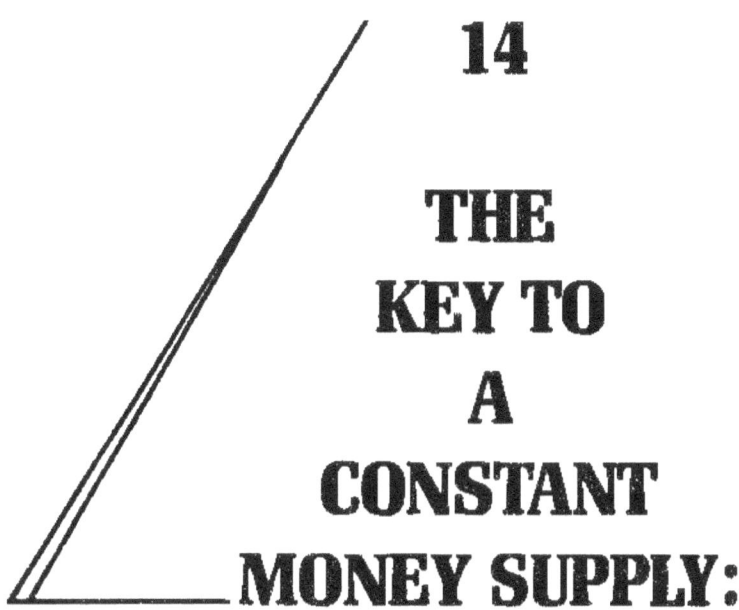

14
THE KEY TO A CONSTANT MONEY SUPPLY:

A warm security blanket through Meta-Cosmic Projection.

If you ever have trouble making ends meet financially, this chapter will be of particular interest to you. The secrets of meta-cosmic projection make it possible for you to have all the money you need when you need it.

The majority of people know what it's like to spend a sleepless night worrying about unpaid bills. If you have never had this experience, count yourself extremely lucky. The emotional pain of not knowing where the money will come from to pay bills when they fall due can often be more uncomfortable than a physical illness. You need never worry about unpaid bills again, thanks to the secrets of meta-cosmic projection given in this chapter. The secrets of meta-cosmic projection can make it possible for you to pay your unpaid bills without a worry.

Man Uses the Secrets of Meta-Cosmic Projection to Pay All His Unpaid Bills

Things looked pretty grim to Mike N. when he came to see me. Mike, a young family man, had been caught in a mass layoff at a local plant. At first unemployment benefits and savings kept the family afloat. As time passed, however, it became obvious to Mike that his available funds could, in no way, cover his family's financial needs. He spent his days searching for a job and his nights figuring out ways to juggle payments in order to appease his creditors.

"I don't know how long I can keep this up," Mike said. "I've been robbing Peter to pay Paul for so long I think I'm getting an ulcer. I've tried every company that might need someone with my qualifications and in each case the answer was 'Sorry, we have no openings.'

"I don't even have a lead on a job. The only thing I have plenty of is unpaid bills and creditors screaming for their money."

Mike was silent for a moment, then he asked, "Will you teach me one of those special techniques so I can get the money to pay my bills? I don't know exactly what they're called, but one of my wife's friends told her something about them. Meta something or other — whatever it was, my wife's friend said it really works. Will you teach that technique to me?"

We talked for an hour or so, and before Mike left, he knew that the "meta something or other" he had asked about was meta-cosmic projection, and he also knew how to use it.

Two weeks later Mike paid another visit.

"If I'm dreaming, please don't wake me up," he said. "That meta-cosmic projection sure works fast. You're not going to believe what happened. Last week a couple pulled into our driveway and asked if we would consider selling our house." A smile filled Mike's face.

"Imagine that!" he said. "We've tried to sell the house three times before and could never get a buyer. There hasn't been a 'for sale' sign up in over a year." Mike grinned again. "They offered us a fantastic price including all our equity in cash in one lump sum. The money they offered in cash was more than enough to pay us completely out of debt and leave enough for a down payment on a house in a subdivision that my wife has wanted to move into for almost two years."

I congratulated Mike on his success and was quickly interrupted by him.

"You haven't heard the half of it yet," Mike grinned. "The guy is with a company just getting a branch going here. When he heard what I had been doing for a living and that I had been laid off he offered me a job with his company. The salary he quoted me is three thousand a year more than I was making before I was laid off.

"The deal on the house is already closed and we move into our new home next month. Next Monday I start my new job. Things couldn't be better. I just wish I had learned about meta-cosmic projection sooner. I could have saved myself a lot of worry and sleepless nights. Anyway, now that I do know about it you can bet it's going to be an active force in my life from here on out."

The last time I heard from Mike he and his family were getting along fine. They loved their new home and Mike really liked his new job. He had made meta-cosmic projection an important part of his daily life and it had given him and his wife a new sense of security.

Mike's story is not exceptional. Meta-cosmic projection has a way of making that which might be considered *exceptional*, seem to be ordinary events of everyday life.

You can begin now to put this powerful technique to work in your life. The secrets of meta-cosmic projection can provide the money you need when you need it.

Man Uses Meta-Cosmic Projection to Get the Money Needed to Have His House Painted

Some people would say that Walt O. didn't really have a serious financial problem. To Walt, however, his problem was a very serious one.

"We have the money we need for basic necessities," said Walt. "I'd like some of the luxuries too. My family deserves them. This might not seem important to you, but my wife wants to have the house painted and I can't afford it. I've looked at our finances from every angle, and the money just isn't there for the paint job she wants."

Walt took a deep breath and continued. "I've heard that you've taught quite a few people some kind of meta-cosmic projection technique to get money when they need it. You might say that I don't really need the money, but I want to get my wife what she wants. She wants the house painted and I *need* money to get it done for her."

No matter what the reason, the secrets of meta-cosmic projection can provide money whenever it is needed. Walt learned the appropriate meta-cosmic projection technique and put it to work immediately.

Three weeks later Walt telephoned. "You ought to bottle that meta-cosmic projection. It works like a charm," he said. "The new paint job looks great. My wife is really happy with it too. You'd think I'd given her a yacht!"

Walt chuckled with pride. "The whole paint job was paid for with cash — in full. Out of the blue I got a chance to do a masonry job that paid me triple-time. The people were really in a hurry. They even paid a bonus for finishing ahead of the time schedule. I even had a few dollars left over after I paid the painters.

"I sure am glad I learned how to use that meta-cosmic projection technique. Believe me, I intend to use it quite a bit in my life."

The meta-cosmic projection technique presented to you in this chapter makes it possible for you to get the money you want when you want it. Don't go another day without the benefits of this powerful technique in your life.

Couple Uses Meta-Cosmic Projection to Pay for Wedding Gifts

Tony and Joyce D. had been married less than a year when they sought my help with a financial problem.

"Please don't tell us that no one expects us to give them a wedding gift," Tony said. "Both my sister and Joyce's brother are getting married next month, and we want to give a wedding gift to each couple. We need a hundred dollars to get the gifts we want to give both of them."

Tony looked at Joyce and smiled. He continued in a low tone.

"Since we're both in school and work only part-time, a hundred dollars sounds like a fortune. We've both heard about a technique you teach people to use to get money when they need it. We'd like you to teach us that technique. We *need* to give those wedding gifts. Call it pride if you want, but it means a lot to both of us."

Joyce and Tony learned quickly. In less than forty-five minutes they knew how to use the secret meta-cosmic projection technique that could get them the money they needed.

"We just had to stop by and thank you," Tony said. "We just bought the wedding gifts we wanted and paid cash for them."

"It's just terrific," said Joyce. "I got a completely unexpected tax refund three days ago. I had added wrong and someone caught it. They corrected my error and sent me a check for one hundred and twenty-one dollars. We treated ourselves to dinner at a nice restaurant, paid for the wedding gifts, and still have two dollars left.

"Thanks again for showing us how to use that meta-cosmic projection technique."

I've received several phone calls from the D's since that day, and each time the purpose of the call was to tell me how meta-cosmic projection had brought them the money they needed when they needed it.

Put that same secret technique to work for you now. You can have the money you need when you need it. The secrets of meta-cosmic projection can work as well for you as they have for countless others. Start today to use the secrets of meta-cosmic projection to fill the financial needs in your own life.

Start Your Own Tuition Fund with the Secrets of Meta-Cosmic Projection

If you have children or grandchildren in college, you already know the cost of higher education. Each day seems to bring new increases in the cost of a college education throughout our nation. It's unfortunate but true that many bright young people, perhaps your own children, grandchildren, nieces or nephews, have been denied a college education due, not to inadequate intelligence, but because of a lack of the large sums of money needed to pay for such an education. Why should a college education be the privilege only of the children of families financially well off? Why shouldn't you and your family have all the money you need when you need it? I can think of no reason to suffer any financial lack in your life. The secrets of meta-cosmic projection are at your fingertips this very moment. Put those secrets to work on your own tuition fund today.

Couple Uses the Secrets of Meta-Cosmic Projection to Send Their Two Children Through College

Before Calvin and Doris G. decided to learn how to use the secrets of meta-cosmic projection they could see no possible way to finance a college education for their two children.

"Our twins will graduate from high school in four months and they both want to go to college," Calvin said. "We encouraged them to apply for admission to a university and they were both accepted. Now it looks as if we'll have to tell them that they just can't go because we can't afford to send them."

The sadness on the faces of both parents was evident.

"Maybe we shouldn't have encouraged them at all," said Doris. "It's hard though, not to want your children to have the good things they want. It may even be impossible. Anyway, Calvin and I want the boys to go to college if there's any way at all we can send them."

Calvin broke into the conversation. "We saw you on TV a couple of weeks ago, and you were talking about some kind of technique that allows a person to get whatever money they need when they need it." Calvin drew in a quick breath and continued. "Believe me, we need money now. Lots of money. About ten thousand dollars.

"I know the boys could have picked a less expensive school, but the way our finances are right now we couldn't afford that either. So if that technique you were talking about works, we might as well go for the school they want. Right?"

"Right!" I agreed.

We settled down to the secrets of meta-cosmic projection.

Calvin and Doris were avid students and learned quickly. In less than an hour they had a clear idea of the meta-cosmic projection technique they were to use to get the money they needed. They left with a promise to keep me posted.

Three full months went by before I heard from the G's. They phoned for a convenient time for another visit. They didn't mention a word about the tuition money over the telephone.

As they walked into my office, their smiles spoke good news. I was taken aback by Calvin's first words.

"Something went wrong. We never got the ten thousand dollars we needed."

My disbelief must have shown on my face, because Doris spoke up quickly.

"Stop teasing, Cal. Tell her the truth."

"Okay. Okay!" Calvin answered. "The truth is, we got more money than we ever dreamed of having. You said the circumstances would present themselves so that we could get the money we needed. Well, did they ever!

"We owned eight acres of land that were considered just about worthless for years. About a month after we started using the meta-cosmic projection technique we were contacted by a real estate developer. He told us that he wanted to buy the land for an apartment complex. When I told him that the land wasn't zoned for apartment buildings, he told me it had been rezoned only one week earlier. Sure enough, we checked and he was right. The land had been rezoned commercial.

"We got a lawyer and he worked the deal out with the land developer. Believe me, we won't have to worry about the twins' tuition money anymore. The deal was closed two days ago.

"The twins can go to medical school, or law school if they want. They have a gigantic tuition fund. Money is no problem now — thanks to that meta-cosmic projection technique."

"He's forgetting to tell you," said Doris, "that we're going to Europe for a whole month. We leave as soon as the boys graduate from high school.

"If anyone had told us four months ago that we'd be giving the twins a vacation in Europe as a graduation present, I'd have thought they were crazy."

Doris smiled at her husband and faced me again.

"We'd like to give you a vacation in Europe as a thank you present. Just let us know when you want to go and we'll take care of everything and bring you your tickets."

Although I appreciated the thought, I assured the G's that no thank you gift was needed. In fact, my policy had always been, and is to this day, to accept only prayers as a token of appreciation. I made it clear that I'd be happy to have all the prayers they were willing to say for me, but trips and other material gifts were out.

"You see," I said, "I practice what I preach. Thanks to meta-cosmic projection, my needs and wants are well taken care of. I have everything I need or want, including all the traveling in this country, Europe, the Middle and Far East, or anywhere else that I can possibly want."

The G's thanked me again and left promising to include me in their prayers.

The secrets of meta-cosmic projection can work just as well for you as they worked for the G's and countless others. You need only follow the flawless meta-cosmic projection techniques given to you in this chapter. Don't waste another minute! Put the secrets of meta-cosmic projection into your life now!

Your Miraculous Meta-Cosmic Projection Technique for Tapping Your Unlimited Money Supply

If you need or want money now, use this miraculous technique three times a day. It is absolutely flawless and can bring you every penny you need and more.

1. *Sit in a relaxed position. Close your eyes.*
2. *For approximately thirty seconds, focus all your at-*

tention on the intake and outflow of your breath without trying to control it.

3. In your own mind and in your own words present your financial needs and wants to your higher self. (For example — "I am in need of money to pay back bills. I need two thousand dollars to bring my bills up to date. In addition I want another five thousand dollars to act as a financial cushion and to give me the money for any extras I might want.")

4. In your own mind see yourself counting the money you need or want. See yourself using the money to fulfill your wants or needs. (For example — See yourself counting out two thousand dollars in one hundred dollar bills. Now see yourself sorting the receipts for your bills marked 'paid in full.' Once you have seen your needs cared for, see yourself counting the money you want for a financial cushion or extras in your life. See yourself buying the things you want. See yourself sitting comfortably, feeling good because you need no longer worry about money.)

5. Now in your mind's eye, see the dollar amount of the total sum you need and/or want. (For example, as in step '3,' see the figure $7,000 clearly in your mind and hold that image for approximately fifteen seconds.)

6. Again, for approximately thirty seconds, focus all your attention on your breathing without attempting to control it.

7. Open your eyes and go about your daily life.

This miraculous secret can change your whole life by making it possible for you to have all the money you need or want. You need never worry about money again. You now have the miraculous meta-cosmic projection technique that allows you to tap your unlimited money supply.

15

YOUR UNLIMITED SUPPLY OF LIFETIME META-COSMIC POWER

You will never experience an energy crisis in the area of meta-cosmic projection. In fact, the more you use these miraculous techniques, the better they work for you. Thousands of people are living proof of this. For a few moments, I want to share a very personal experience with you.

Before I was cured by metaphysical healing of blindness, epilepsy and paralysis, things looked pretty bleak for me. It seemed no one would even consider hiring me for volunteer work, let alone gainful employment. I had less than a snowball's chance in a furnace of ever being financially self-supporting, let alone financially secure. I was dependent on others for money, for transportation, for reading, for shopping, and for the everyday things in life which most people take for granted. In many ways I found that dependency almost as painful as my physical handicaps. It seemed I would never have a chance to "make my mark" on the world, to leave it a little better for my having lived. Then I discovered the secrets of Meta-Cosmic Projection.

My book, *The Miracle of Metaphysical Healing,* tells how I healed my physical handicaps and my limited thinking. I then began to search for the techniques that would allow me to accomplish my goals. I needed techniques that wouldn't take forever to work. After all, I had already wasted nine years of life in the torment of blindness, epilepsy and paralysis. I didn't want to lose even one additional minute. I had vowed to share the miracle of metaphysical healing with the world, but the world wasn't knocking at my door to ask for that miracle. As much as any general facing a battle, I needed a plan of action. After much soul searching, meditation and prayer, I found that plan — The Secrets of Meta-Cosmic Projection! There was never a doubt in my mind that meta-cosmic projection would work. How could it fail? The secrets of meta-cosmic projection underlie all reality.

With the very same miraculous techniques that are now yours, I set out to gain whatever I would need to share the miracle of meta-physical healing with all of mankind. I used the secrets of meta-cosmic projection to gain the contacts I would need to keep the vow I had made.

In just a short time I was contacted by Georgia State University and asked to teach a course in parapsychology and the power of the mind. Only a few short weeks later, *The Atlanta Constitution* newspaper asked to do an article on me and my work. Meta-cosmic projection was working its miracles and it worked them quickly. Local TV and radio stations asked me to appear on their various shows. Not long after that, *Newsweek* magazine featured a story on me in its educational section. This was followed by mention of my work in *Time* magazine. There was just no stopping the limitless power of meta-cosmic projection. Soon I was receiving requests to appear on national TV, also TV and radio shows throughout the United States and Canada. Perhaps you saw my appearance on the David Suskind Show, Tom Snyder's Tomorrow Show, or the Mike Douglas Show. Maybe you read about my work in the *National Inquirer, Midnight, New Dimension Magazine, Science of Mind* magazine, *Cosmopolitan* magazine, or *New Woman* magazine. Brad Steiger has mentioned me and my work in his writings, and *The Journal of Osteopathic Medicine* has also devoted an article to my work in healing, as has the *Journal of Rehabilitation.*

Through the miracle of meta-cosmic projection I have spoken by invitation at numerous seminars dealing with nontraditional healing, including a New Dimensions in Healing workshop conducted by a medical school in Florida, an all-day seminar at the School of Osteopathic Medicine, and a five-day workshop at the Blic Clinic in Ohio.

The identical miraculous techniques of meta-cosmic projection that I used to reach my goals are at your fingertips now. They enabled me to have my articles published in Canadian and U.S. magazines and to receive a teaching appointment at the Emory University School of Nursing where I instructed senior nursing students in the power and use of the mind.

Thanks to the secrets of meta-cosmic projection, my first book, *Put Your Psychic Powers to Work,* and my second book, *The Miracle of Metaphysical Healing,* were published. *The Miracle of Metaphysical Healing* is now published in translation in Germany.

The secrets of meta-cosmic projection have enabled me to attain and obtain everything I want or need and they can do the same for you. There is no stopping the limitless power they place within your reach. They reach into the past, the present and create the future you want. Soon the *New Guide to Metaphysical Healing* will be published and will be available to you. No one should be without the miraculous secrets of meta-cosmic projection that put all things within the reach of each person. It was for this reason that I wrote this book. You deserve to have these miraculous secrets at work in your life this very day.

Man Teaches His Friends the Secrets of Meta-Cosmic Projection

Robert Z. was determined to share the secrets of meta-cosmic projection with his friends and loved ones. Robert had used the fabulous secrets only two weeks when he decided to teach his loved ones to put them to work in their lives.

"I knew that meta-cosmic projection worked," said Robert. "I decided it was too good to keep to myself so I began to talk about the secrets to my family and friends. In just a matter of weeks I was getting reports from friends and relatives on how meta-cosmic projection had worked for them.

"One of my friends, who had been out of work for months, used it to get a job. He got exactly the job he wanted and it only took him twelve days with meta-cosmic projection." Robert smiled and continued. "My niece used it to get accepted in college and my nephew used meta-cosmic projection to get the car he had wanted for six months."

To say that Robert is sold on meta-cosmic projection is to put it mildly.

"Everyone should know the secrets of meta-cosmic projection. Why don't you write a book explaining how people can use them in every area of their life?"

Meta-Cosmic Projection Works for the Material and the Intangible

No matter what your goals, the secrets of meta-cosmic projection can put them within your reach now. The more you use those miraculous secrets the better they work for you.

Katherine B. learned this fact very quickly. She had tried everything to get her family back together and everything had failed. Her two sons and her husband didn't speak and the boys had left home, for Katherine knew not where.

"It's just awful," said Katherine. "My sons and their father love each other but a stupid argument has been blown all out of proportion and each is unwilling to say he's sorry.

"In addition to my family being broken up, our house is in sad shape. There was a fire two weeks ago and the furniture was ruined by smoke and water damage. The house is fine but it's just about without furniture. I can't even hope my husband will consider making up with the boys while he's so worried about refurnishing the house. Unfortunately we had no insurance and we just can't afford new furniture. Ken is really worried sick."

Katherine looked me directly in the eyes.

"Will you teach me those meta-cosmic projection techniques I've heard you mention? I can't really see any way out of this mess, but if those secrets work as well as you say they do, I'd sure like to give them a try. I have nothing to lose and an awful lot to gain."

Katherine learned quickly and left vowing to refurnish her home and reunite her family with the secrets of meta-cosmic projection.

In just four weeks Katherine was back for another visit.

"I can't thank you enough for teaching me how to use meta-cosmic projection," Katherine bubbled. "Believe it or not our whole house is completely refurnished. Ken got an unexpected bonus, and we found a terrific sale on exactly the new furniture we needed.

"Even more important, though," Katherine went on, "our sons are back home. The entire disagreement between Ken and the boys has been cleared up and I have my family back together again — all thanks to the secrets of meta-cosmic projection. Believe me, meta-cosmic projection will be part of our life from now on."

Meta-Cosmic Projection Can Only Be Used for Good

Despite the fact that I always tell people that the secrets of meta-cosmic projection can only be used for good, there are a few people who seem determined to learn this the hard way. Jeff L. was one such person.

Jeff had one predominant problem in the front of his mind when he sought my help. For one year Jeff had looked forward to a managerial promotion with his company.

"The thing just hasn't come through," said Jeff. "I know exactly what's blocking it, but I don't know how to get around it. I figured maybe the meta-cosmic projection thing you teach could help me get rid of the guy who has the job I want."

That was all I needed to launch into all the reasons why meta-cosmic projection could not be used to "get rid" of anybody.

"I can teach you to use meta-cosmic projection to help your self, but believe me it can't be used against anyone without falling on your own head," I said. "Do you want to learn to use it for your good?"

Jeff thought for a moment.

"Yeah, I guess so," he said. "It just seems more logical to get rid of this guy. He's all that's in my way."

"Jeff, there's no way I'm going to teach you meta-cosmic projection to do harm to anyone. If you want to use it for yourself fine, but I would want your word not to try to use meta-cosmic projection to do anyone harm."

"Okay, you have my word," said Jeff. "All I want is that job. I won't use what you teach me to try to hurt anyone."

Jeff learned the secrets of meta-cosmic projection and left to go after his promotion. One month later he was back in my office.

"I know I should have listened to you, but I thought I could speed things up. I used the technique you taught me to try to get the guy fired. The way I figured it, I was a cinch to get the job once it was open."

Jeff paused briefly and his face clouded over. "The guy didn't get fired — I did," said Jeff. "They just told me I wasn't needed any more. No explanation, no nothing.

"I've been looking for a job for a week but I haven't been able to find one. Can you help me? Will you teach me how to use meta-cosmic projection to find a new job? Honest, I've learned my lesson."

It took Jeff another hour to convince me that he had learned through his experience. After an additional forty minutes, Jeff left with another meta-cosmic projection technique.

Two weeks passed before I received a call from Jeff.

"I started my new job last week," he said. "That technique sure does work fast, and it really works great too. This job is exactly what I've always wanted. I'm sorry I had to learn the hard way, but believe me I have learned my lesson. Meta-cosmic projection is going to have a regular place in my life, but I'll use it only for good."

I'm happy to report that the people who learn the hard way are few and far between. The secrets of meta-cosmic projection are yours to use today, but remember, they can be used only for good! Any attempt to use meta-cosmic projection to harm anyone will only result in tragedy for the person using the techniques wrongfully.

Share Meta-Cosmic Projection and Bring Gains to Yourself

It's a pleasant fact that the more you share the secrets of meta-cosmic projection, the more good you gain for yourself. When you share these miraculous secrets, you set up a chain reaction that continues to send good things to you. When you give these secrets as a gift to another, you assure yourself of doubled and redoubled gifts as a result of your action.

Begin to use the secrets of meta-cosmic projection today. Use these miraculous secrets for yourself, and share them with your family and friends. You can rest assured that not only will you achieve your goals, but you will also derive special gifts through the act of sharing with others.

Don't wait another minute. The miraculous secrets of meta-cosmic projection are available to you now. Begin to use and share the unlimited power of meta-cosmic projection today, then sit back and watch the good in your life multiply!

OTHER INSPIRATIONAL AND METAPHYSICAL BOOKS FROM PARKER PUBLISHING COMPANY

- The Cosmic Power Within You, Joseph Murphy
- Infinite Power for Richer Living, Joseph Murphy
- Miracle Power for Infinite Riches, Joseph Murphy
- The Mystic Path to Cosmic Power, Vernon Howard
- The Power of Miracle Metaphysics, Robert B. Stone
- The Power of Your Subconscious Mind, Joseph Murphy
- Secrets of the I-Ching, Joseph Murphy
- Secrets of Mental Magic, Vernon Howard
- Telecult Power: Amazing New Way to Psychic and Occult Wonders, Reese P. Dubin
- Your Infinite Power to Be Rich, Joseph Murphy

www.parkerpub.co

www.ingramcontent.com/pod-product-compliance
Lightning Source LLC
Chambersburg PA
CBHW021406290426
44108CB00010B/404